Fairfield P.N.E.U. School
(Backwell) Ltd.,
Farleigh Road,
Backwell, Bristol.

821

He Said, She Said, They Said

POETRY IN CONVERSATION

Other poetry collections edited by Anne Harvey
IN TIME OF WAR
A PICNIC OF POETRY
OCCASIONS
THE LANGUAGE OF LOVE

Poetry Originals
THE MAGNIFICENT CALLISTO   Gerard Benson
TWO'S COMPANY   Jackie Kay

BLACKIE CHILDREN'S BOOKS

Published by the Penguin Group
Penguin Books Ltd, 27 Wrights Lane, London W8 5TZ, England
Penguin Books USA Inc., 375 Hudson Street, New York, NY 10014, USA
Penguin Books Australia Ltd, Ringwood, Victoria, Australia
Penguin Books Canada Ltd, 10 Alcorn Avenue, Toronto, Ontario, Canada M4V 3B2
Penguin Books (NZ) Ltd, 182-190 Wairau Road, Auckland 10, New Zealand

Penguin Books Ltd, Registered Offices: Harmondsworth, Middlesex, England

First published 1993
1 3 5 7 9 10 8 6 4 2
First edition

Introduction copyright © Anne Harvey, 1993
This selection copyright © Anne Harvey, 1993
Illustrations copyright © Amanda Hall, 1993

The Acknowledgements on pp.156-159 constitute an extension of this copyright page

All rights reserved. Without limiting the rights under copyright reserved above, no part of this publication may be reproduced, stored in or introduced into a retrieval system, or transmitted, in any form or by any means (electronic, mechanical, photocopying, recording or otherwise), without the prior written permission of both the copyright owner and the above publisher of this book.

Filmset in 12/14pt Linotype Baskerville
by Rowland Phototypesetting Ltd
Bury St Edmunds, Suffolk
Printed in England by Clays Ltd, St Ives plc

A CIP catalogue record for this book is available from the British Library

ISBN 0 216-94023-0

He Said, She Said, They Said

POETRY IN CONVERSATION

Edited by Anne Harvey

Illustrated by Amanda Hall

Blackie Children's Books

Contents

Introduction .... *Anne Harvey*   9

Conversations

Meet-on-the-Road .... *Anon*   10
Lost and Found .... *Richard Edwards*   12
Are You Receiving Me? .... *Margaret Porter*   14
Meeting Mary .... *Eleanor Farjeon*   16
Bunches of Grapes .... *Walter de la Mare*   17
Mary, Mary Magdalene .... *Charles Causley*   18
Conversation .... *Olive Dove*   20
Brother and Sister .... *Lewis Carroll*   22
Soldier, Soldier .... *Anon*   23
O What Is That Sound .... *W.H. Auden*   24
Café Conversation .... *Richard Edwards*   26
The Telephone .... *Robert Frost*   27
Early Evening Quarrel .... *Langston Hughes*   28
Teevee .... *Eve Merriam*   29
Madam and the Rent Man ...... *Langston Hughes*   30
999 .... *Maurice Lindsay*   32
Fire! Fire! .... *Traditional*   33
Ruth Luce and Bruce Booth ...... *N.M. Bodecker*   34
Mr Jones .... *Harry Graham*   34
Overheard in a Doctor's Waiting-room ....
.... *Gerard Benson*   34
What's the Problem? .... *Ian Serraillier*   35
The Well-wrought Urn .... *Irving Layton*   36
Interview with a Poet .... *Miroslav Holub*   37

Youth, Age and Poetry: A Dialogue .... *Vernon Scannell* 38
In the East .... *Archibald MacLeish* 39
Vermont Conversation .... *Patricia Hubbell* 40
Studup .... *Barrie Wade* 41
Daydreamer .... *David Durham* 42
The Traveller .... *Raymond Wilson* 43

Talk to the Animals

Dialogue Between My Cat Bridget and Me .... *Kit Wright* 44
Cows .... *James Reeves* 46
Little Piggy .... *Thomas Hood* 48
On a Night of Snow .... *Elizabeth Coatsworth* 49
This and That .... *Gareth Owen* 49
To My Dog Brock .... *David King* 52
It Is I, the Little Owl .... *Chippewa Indian* 53
Raccoon .... *William Jay Smith* 54
The Tickle Rhyme .... *Ian Serraillier* 56
The Flamingo .... *Lewis Gaylord Clark* 56
David and Goliath .... *Catherine Benson* 58
Catching a Carp .... *Jan Dean* 59
The Barn .... *Elizabeth Coatsworth* 60
'I,' Said the Donkey .... *Anon* 62
Noah and the Rabbit .... *Hugh Chesterman* 63
A Footprint on the Air .... *Naomi Lewis* 64

Ghostly Gossip

Green Candles	*Humbert Wolfe*	65
Who's in the Next Room?	*Thomas Hardy*	66
Johnny Dow	*Anon*	67
Bones	*Walter de la Mare*	67
Grave Talk	*Raymond Wilson*	68
Ghosts	*Kit Wright*	70
We Are Seven	*William Wordsworth*	71
Unwelcome Guest	*Clive Sansom*	74
A Frosty Night	*Robert Graves*	75
from Little Mary Crosbie	*Margaret Cropper*	77
Her-zie	*Stevie Smith*	78
Overheard on a Saltmarsh	*Harold Monro*	79
The Two Rivers	*Anon*	80
Gargoyles	*Clive Sansom*	80
Hallowe'en	*Marie A. Lawson*	82
Witch, Witch	*Rose Fyleman*	83
The Witches, from *Macbeth*	*William Shakespeare*	84
Let Us In	*Olive Dove*	86
The Night Express	*Frances Cornford*	87

Imagine That

The Toys Talk of the World	*Katharine Pyle*	88
The Table and the Chair	*Edward Lear*	90
The Lady of Shalots	*Reginald Arkell*	92
Jam	*David McCord*	93
Cross Purposes	*Mrs Richard Strachey*	94
My True Love	*Ivy O. Eastwick*	95
There Was a Lady Loved a Swine	*Anon*	96
Lanky Lee and Lindy Lou	*Colin West*	97

If I Were a Queen .... *Christina Rossetti*	97
The Flattered Flying-Fish .... *E.V. Rieu*	98
Johnny Sands .... *Anon*	98
My Very Peculiar Pet .... *Hannah McBain*	100
The First Men on Mercury .... *Edwin Morgan*	102
How to Treat Elves .... *Morris Bishop*	104
Some Curious Habits of Jonathan Bing	
.... *Beatrice Curtis Brown*	106
You Can't Be That .... *Brian Patten*	108
Storytime .... *Judith Nicholls*	110

Words on the Wind

The Tree and the Wind .... *Robin Mellor*	112
Old Man Ocean .... *Russell Hoban*	114
Once the Wind .... *Shake Keane*	115
The West Wind .... *John Masefield*	116
Lady Moon .... *Lord Houghton*	118
Day and Night .... *Lady Anne Lindsay*	119
A Conversation, from *Under Milk Wood*	
.... *Dylan Thomas*	120
Song .... *Elizabeth Coatsworth*	121
Christmas Scandal .... *William Kean Seymour*	122
Snowman's Land .... *Florence Harrison*	124
What Is Pink? .... *Christina Rossetti*	125
The Clod and the Pebble .... *William Blake*	126
The Tree and the Pool .... *Brian Patten*	127
Waiting Both .... *Thomas Hardy*	128
Heaven .... *George Herbert*	129

What the Parents Said

Father and I in the Woods	*David McCord*	130
A Lot to Ask	*John Latham*	131
The Avaricious Boy	*Colin West*	132
A Conversation Overheard	*Anon*	133
What Did You Learn in School Today	*Tom Paxton*	134
Tell Me Why?	*Roger McGough*	136
'Father, May I Go to War?'	*Anon*	137
'Mother, May I Take a Swim?'	*Anon*	137
Distracted the Mother Said to Her Boy	*Gregory Harrison*	138
Don't Go Through That Revolving Door	*Anon*	138
My Dad, Your Dad	*Kit Wright*	139
The Good Little Girl	*A.A. Milne*	140
The Spider	*Jane Taylor*	141
A Girl's Questions	*Wes Magee*	142
Slow Thaw	*Ian McMillan*	143
This Morning	*Jon Stallworthy*	144
Little Abigail and the Beautiful Pony	*Shel Silverstein*	146
Sailor	*Meg Seaton*	148
Vision and Late Supper	*Nancy Willard*	149
From a Very Little Sphinx	*Edna St Vincent Millay*	151
The Room	*Frances Bellerby*	152
The Sick Child	*Robert Louis Stevenson*	153
Uphill	*Christina Rossetti*	154
Acknowledgements		156

*I*ntroduction

Where did the idea spring from? What made me spend nearly two years searching for poems written in conversation? It could have been a poetry day in a school where I realized how much the children had enjoyed reading out poems in twos, threes and groups. Or perhaps I was recalling a rather special drama group I once ran, the Wednesday Group – nine enthusiastic young actors and speakers who put on plays, arranged programmes and knew how to lift poems off the printed page and bring them imaginatively alive. Maybe my memory was going further back, into my own childhood, when poetry was one of my favourite lessons. Our teacher divided us into pairs, trios or groups for speaking the Robin Hood ballads, or Edward Lear's marvellous nonsense, or – the one that really stands out – Harold Monro's 'Overheard on a Saltmarsh'. I still remember how the wooden desks and chairs, the cream-walled classroom and the uniformed pupils vanished as the poem's haunting, mocking atmosphere took over. I was chosen to be the rather proud, teasing and possessive nymph, but secretly longed to be the greedy, persistent goblin. Since then I've met many people, poets among them, who were first introduced to that poem at school, and friends hearing about this book invariably suggested: 'Oh, you must use "Overheard on . . ."' 'Yes, thank you,' I agreed. 'I shall.'

There seemed to be a wide choice for poems written in character – animals talk together, and so do ghosts, parents and children, brothers and sisters, trees, birds, winds and seas – and in many different styles, shapes and moods. Some need a narrator and some don't. Experiment with them, try them out in different ways, alter your voice to suit the subject and character expressively, discover how they best work. The poems could be used at school in your poetry lesson, or for an assembly or concert, or at home if you and your family or friends are making your own entertainment – perhaps for a party, or to raise money for a charity.

I've enjoyed compiling this collection, reading through old books for unusual poems, trying them out on school Book Week visits for 'second opinions' – and sometimes asking rather puzzled guests (who thought they had come for a chat or a coffee) to speak them aloud with me.

And now it's your turn to discover exactly what 'He said', 'She said', and 'They said' for yourselves . . .

Conversations

Meet-on-the-Road

'Now pray, where are you going, child?' said
  Meet-on-the-Road.
'To school, sir, to school, sir,' said
  Child-as-it-Stood.
'What have you got in your basket, child?' said
  Meet-on-the-Road.
'My dinner, sir, my dinner, sir,' said
  Child-as-it-Stood.
'What have you for your dinner, child?' said
  Meet-on-the-Road.
'Some pudding, sir, some pudding, sir,' said
  Child-as-it-Stood.

'Oh then, I pray, give me a share,' said
    Meet-on-the-Road.
'I've little enough for myself, sir,' said
    Child-as-it-Stood.
'What have you got that cloak on for?' said
    Meet-on-the-Road.
'To keep the wind and the cold from me,' said
    Child-as-it-Stood.
'I wish the wind would blow through you,' said
    Meet-on-the-Road.
'Oh, what a wish! Oh, what a wish!' said
    Child-as-it-Stood.
'Pray, what are those bells ringing for?' said
    Meet-on-the-Road.
'To ring bad spirits home again,' said
    Child-as-it-Stood.
'Oh, then I must be going, child!' said
    Meet-on-the-Road.
'So fare you well, so fare you well,' said
    Child-as-it-Stood.

ANON

Lost and Found

I was worrying over some homework
When my Grandad walked into the room
And sat wearily down with a grunt and a frown
And a face full of sorrow and gloom.

'I've lost it, I've lost it,' he muttered,
'And it's very important to me.'
'Lost what?' I replied. 'I've forgotten,' he sighed,
'But it's something beginning with T.'

'A toffee, perhaps,' I suggested,
'Or a teapot or even your tie,
Or some toast or a thread . . .' but he shook his grey head
As a tear trickled out of one eye.

'A tuba,' I said, 'or some treacle,
Or a toggle to sew on your mac,
Or a tray or a ticket, a tree or a thicket,
A thistle, a taper, a tack.'

But Grandad looked blank. 'Well, some tweezers,
Or a theory,' I said, 'or a tooth,
Or a tap or a till or thought or a thrill
Or your trousers, a trestle, the truth.'

'It's none of those things,' grumbled Grandad.
'A toy trumpet,' I offered, 'a towel,
Or a trout, a tureen, an antique tambourine,
A toboggan, a tortoise, a trowel . . . '

Then suddenly Grandad's scowl vanished,
'I've remembered!' he cried with a shout.
'It's my temper, you brat, so come here and take that!'
And he boxed both my ears and stalked out.

RICHARD EDWARDS

Are You Receiving Me?

'How's Auntie? Feeling the cold?'

'Old? You don't think I'm old?
I'm a young eighty-nine
And most of the time
I'm like a spring lamb in the fold!'

'It's good that you're hale and hearty.'

'Party? Who's having a party?
Not quite my thing,
Hope it goes with a swing,
But I find all your friends a bit arty!'

'We thought we'd come for the day.'

'Stay? You can't come and stay.
I've scrapped the spare bed,
Come for supper instead;
I'm sure you remember the way.'

'I'll bring you a bunch of flowers.'

'Showers? Did you say showers?
For this time of year
It's incredibly clear;
No sign of a cloud for some hours!'

'Oh and Jo has passed her exam.'

'Pram? You've bought a new pram?
That's wonderful news,
You all know my views!
I can't say how delighted I am!'

'Goodbye, then – and love to the cat!'

'Flat? I don't live in a flat!
(My niece is devoted,
But lately I've noted
She's developed this odd line in chat!)'

MARGARET PORTER

Meeting Mary

Hard by the Wildbrooks I met Mary,
When berries smelled sweet and hot.
Mary, I fancy, was seven years old,
And I am never mind what.

'What are you getting?' I asked Mary.
'Blackberries. What are you?'
'Toadflax,' I answered Mary, 'and mushrooms.'
'How many mushrooms?' 'Two.'

'Going to have blackberries stewed for dinner,
Or blackberry jam?' said I.
'Not goin' to have neither,' said Mary;
'Goin' to have blackberry pie.'

'Aren't you lucky!' I said to Mary.
'And what sort of name have you got?'
'*My* name's Mary,' said Mary, 'what's *your* name?'
I told her never mind what.

'Good-bye, Mary,' 'Good-bye,' said Mary,
And went on picking and eating.
That's all about my meeting with Mary –
It's my favourite sort of meeting.

ELEANOR FARJEON

CONVERSATIONS

Bunches of Grapes

'Bunches of grapes,' says Timothy;
'Pomegranates pink,' says Elaine;
'A junket of cream and a cranberry tart
   For me,' says Jane.

'Love-in-a-mist,' says Timothy;
'Primroses pale,' said Elaine;
'A nosegay of pinks and mignonette
   For me,' says Jane.

'Chariots of gold,' says Timothy;
'Silvery wings,' says Elaine;
'A bumpity ride in a wagon of hay
   For me,' says Jane.

WALTER DE LA MARE

Mary, Mary Magdalene

On the east wall of the church of St Mary Magdalene at Launceston in Cornwall is a granite figure of the saint. The children of the town say that a stone lodged on her back will bring good luck.

Mary, Mary Magdalene
Lying on the wall,
I throw a pebble on your back.
Will it lie or fall?

Send me down for Christmas
Some stockings and some hose,
And send before the winter's end
A brand-new suit of clothes.

Mary, Mary Magdalene
Under a stony tree,
I throw a pebble on your back.
What will you send me?

I'll send you for your christening
A woollen robe to wear,
A shiny cup from which to sup,
And a name to bear.

Mary, Mary Magdalene
Lying cool as snow,
What will you be sending me
When to school I go?

> *I'll send a pencil and a pen*
> *That write both clean and neat,*
> *And I'll send to the schoolmaster*
> *A tongue that's kind and sweet.*

Mary, Mary Magdalene
Lying in the sun,
What will you be sending me
Now I'm twenty-one?

> *I'll send you down a locket*
> *As silver as your skin,*
> *And I'll send you a lover*
> *To fit a gold key in.*

Mary, Mary Magdalene
Underneath the spray,
What will you be sending me
On my wedding-day?

> *I'll send you down some blossom,*
> *Some ribbon and some lace,*
> *And for the bride a veil to hide*
> *The blushes on her face.*

Mary, Mary Magdalene
Whiter than the swan,
Tell me what you'll send me,
Now my good man's dead and gone.

> *I'll send to you a single bed*
> *On which you must lie,*
> *And pillows bright where tears may light*
> *That fall from your eye.*

Mary, Mary Magdalene
Now nine months are done,
What will you be sending me
For my little son?

> *I'll send you for your baby*
> *A lucky stone, and small,*
> *To throw to Mary Magdalene*
> *Lying on the wall.*

CHARLES CAUSLEY

Conversation

Why are you always tagging on?
You ought to be dressing dolls
Like other sisters.

Dolls! You know I don't like them.
Cold, stiff things lying so still.
Let's go to the woods and climb trees.
The crooked elm is the best.

From the top you can see the river
And the old man hills,
Hump-backed and hungry
As ragged beggars.
In the day they seem small and far away
But at night they crowd closer
And stand like frowning giants.
Come on! What are you waiting for?

I have better things do to.

It's wild in the woods today.
Rooks claw the air with their cackling.
The trees creak and sigh.
They say that long ago, slow Sam the woodcutter
Who liked to sleep in the hollow oak,
Was found dead there.
The sighing is his ghost, crying to come back.
Let's go and hear it.

I hate the sound.

You mean you're afraid?

Of course not.
Jim and I are going fishing.

Can I come too?

What do you know about fishing?
You're only a girl.

OLIVE DOVE

Brother and Sister

'Sister, sister, go to bed!
Go and rest your weary head.'
Thus the prudent brother said.

'Do you want a battered hide,
Or scratches to your face applied?'
Thus his sister calm replied.

'Sister, do not raise my wrath.
I'd make you into mutton broth
As easily as kill a moth!'

The sister raised her beaming eye
And looked on him indignantly
And sternly answered, 'Only try!'

Off to the cook he quickly ran.
'Dear Cook, please lend a frying-pan
To me as quickly as you can.'

'And wherefore should I lend it you?'
'The reason, Cook, is plain to view.
I wish to make an Irish stew.'

'What meat is in that stew to go?'
'My sister'll be the contents!'
                                'Oh!'
'You'll lend the pan to me, Cook?'
                                'No!'

Moral: Never stew your sister.

LEWIS CARROLL

Soldier, Soldier

'Oh! Soldier, soldier, won't you marry me,
   With your musket, fife and drum?'
'*Oh no, sweet maid, I cannot marry thee,*
   For I have no coat to put on.'

So up she went to her grandfather's chest,
And she got him a coat of the very, very best
   And the soldier put it on!

'Oh! Soldier, soldier, won't you marry me,
   With your musket, fife and drum?'
'*Oh no, sweet maid, I cannot marry thee,*
   For I have no hat to put on.'

So up she went to her grandfather's chest,
And she got him a hat of the very, very best
   And the soldier put it on!

'Oh! Soldier, soldier, won't you marry me,
   With your musket, fife and drum?'
'*Oh no, sweet maid, I cannot marry thee,*
   For I have no boots to put on.'

So up she went to her grandfather's chest,
And she got him a pair of the very, very best
   And the soldier put them on!

'Oh! Soldier, soldier, won't you marry me,
   With your musket, fife and drum?'
'*Oh no, sweet maid, I cannot marry thee,*
   For I have a wife of my own!'

ANON

O What Is That Sound

O what is that sound which so thrills the ear
   Down in the valley drumming, drumming?
Only the scarlet soldiers, dear,
   The soldiers coming.

O what is that light I see flashing so clear
   Over the distance brightly, brightly?
Only the sun on their weapons, dear,
   As they step lightly.

O what are they doing with all that gear,
   What are they doing this morning, this morning?
Only their usual manoeuvres, dear,
   Or perhaps a warning.

O why have they left the road down there,
   Why are they suddenly wheeling, wheeling?
Perhaps a change in their orders, dear.
   Why are you kneeling?

O haven't they stopped for the doctor's care,
   Haven't they reined their horses, their horses?
Why, they are none of them wounded, dear,
   None of these forces.

O is it the parson they want, with white hair,
   Is it the parson, is it, is it?
No, they are passing his gateway, dear,
   Without a visit.

CONVERSATIONS

O it must be the farmer who lives so near.
   It must be the farmer so cunning, so cunning?
They have passed the farmyard already, dear,
   And now they are running.

O where are you going? Stay with me here!
   Were the vows you swore deceiving, deceiving?
No, I promised to love you, dear,
   But I must be leaving.

O it's broken the lock and splintered the door,
   O it's the gate where they're turning, turning;
Their boots are heavy on the floor
   And their eyes are burning.

W. H. AUDEN

Café Conversation

'Oo-er! A nasty maggot thing!'
Shrieked poor short-sighted Mabel,
But I shook my head and I answered, 'No
It's a bread-crumb on the table.'

'Look!' Mabel gulped, 'That woman's got
A squirrel on her head!'
But I shook my head, 'A squirrel indeed!
It's a furry hat,' I said.

'Be careful! There's a cobra on
That chair back!' Mabel cried.
But I shook my head, 'It isn't a snake,
It's my school scarf,' I replied.

Then Mabel's eyes gazed into mine
And this is what I heard:
'I think you're the handsomest boy in the room.'
I didn't say a word.

RICHARD EDWARDS

The Telephone

'When I was just as far as I could walk
From here today,
There was an hour
All still
When leaning with my head against a flower
I heard you talk.
Don't say I didn't, for I heard you say –
You spoke from that flower on the windowsill –
Do you remember what it was you said?'

'First tell me what it was you thought you heard.'

'Having found the flower and driven a bee away,
I leaned my head,
And holding by the stalk,
I listened and I thought I caught the word –
What was it? Did you call me by my name?
Or did you say –
Someone said "Come" – I heard it as I bowed.'

'I may have thought as much, but not aloud.'

'Well, so I came.'

ROBERT FROST

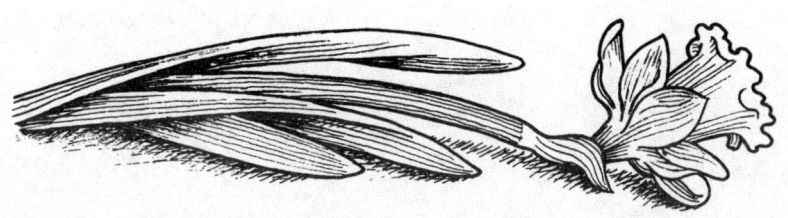

Early Evening Quarrel

Where is that sugar, Hammond,
I sent you this morning to buy?
I say, where is that sugar
I sent you this morning to buy?
Coffee without sugar
Makes a good woman cry.

> *I ain't got no sugar, Hattie,*
> *I gambled your dime away.*
> *Ain't got no sugar, I*
> *Done gambled that dime away.*
> *If you's a wise woman, Hattie,*
> *You ain't gonna have nothin to say.*

I ain't no wise woman, Hammond.
I am evil and mad.
Ain't no sense in a good woman
Bein treated so bad.

> *I don't treat you bad, Hattie,*
> *Neither does I treat you good.*
> *But I reckon I could treat you*
> *Worser if I would.*

Lawd, these things we women
Have to stand!
I wonder is there nowhere a
Do-right man?

LANGSTON HUGHES

Teevee

In the house
of Mr and Mrs Spouse
he and she
would watch teevee
and never a word
between them spoken
until the day
the set was broken.

Then 'How do you do?'
said he to she,
'I don't believe
that we've met yet.
Spouse is my name,
What's yours?' he asked.

'Why mine's the same!'
said she to he,
'Do you suppose that we could be – ?'

But the set came suddenly right about,
and so they never did find out.

EVE MERRIAM

Madam and the Rent Man

The rent man knocked.
He said, Howdy-do?
I said, What
Can I do for you?
He said, You know
Your rent is due?

> I said, Listen,
> Before I'd pay
> I'd go to Hades
> And rot away!
>
> The sink is broke,
> The water don't run,
> And you ain't done a thing
> You promised to've done.
>
> Back window's cracked,
> Kitchen floor squeaks,
> There's rats in the cellar,
> And the attic leaks.

> > He said, Madam,
> > It's not up to me.
> > I'm just the agent,
> > Don't you see?

CONVERSATIONS

I said, Naturally,
You pass the buck.
If it's money you want
You're out of luck.

> He said, Madam,
> I ain't pleased!
> I said, Neither am I.

>> So we agrees!

LANGSTON HUGHES

999

Is that the Fire Brigade?
Yes, the Fire Brigade.
Where's the fire?
There isn't a fire. It's water.
Water?
Yes, water. Coming through the roof in seventeen places.
We're being flooded. Please can you come and help us?
A waterfall. It's pouring down the stairs like Niagara.
What's fallen?
Water.
But we're the Fire Brigade.
I know you're the Fire Brigade. But I've seen on the telly
you rescuing flooded-out people with boats. *Yes, we do that.
But you're at the top of a hill. You can't get boats there.*
I know you can't. But, I tell you, we're being flooded.
We need your help. *If it isn't a case for boats, then
I'll speak to the Superintendent and ring you back . . .*
. . . Is that the Fire Brigade ringing back?
Yes, the Fire Brigade.
Are you coming to help?
*Well, no, I'm afraid we're not.
If your cat got stuck up a tree, or the dog on the roof,
or, of course, you'd an actual fire . . .*
I'll put him there.
Put who where?
The dog on the roof.

> *Oh, you can't do that!*
He'd have to get there by himself. What the hell's that noise?
I'm sticking the cat up a . . .
> *Look, you'd better get off*
the line, chum. Some folk's maybe in serious trouble.

MAURICE LINDSAY

Fire! Fire!

'Fire, fire!'
Said Mrs McGuire.
'Where, where?'
Said Mrs Ware.
'Downtown!'
Said Mrs Brown.
'Heaven save us!'
Said Mrs Davis.

TRADITIONAL

CONVERSATIONS

Ruth Luce and Bruce Booth

Said little Ruth Luce
to little Bruce Booth:
'Lithen,' said Ruth,
'I've a little looth tooth!'

Said little Bruce Booth:
'Tho what if you do?
that'th nothing thpethial –
I've a looth tooth too!'

N. M. BODECKER

Mr Jones

'There's been an accident!' they said,
'Your servant's cut in half; he's dead!'
'Indeed!' said Mr Jones, 'and please
Send me the half that's got my keys.'

HARRY GRAHAM

Overheard in a Doctor's Waiting-room

'Ha! Taking a week off?'
'Heart aching, a wee cough.'

GERARD BENSON

34

CONVERSATIONS

What's the Problem?

'Doctor, I'm very low,' the old man said.
   'What do you advise?'

'Get out and about, enjoy yourself –
   That would be wise;
There's a circus in town –
Go and see Grock, the great clown,
   He'll make you laugh.'

'I am Grock.'

IAN SERRAILLIER

The Well-wrought Urn

'What would you do
if I suddenly died?'

'Write a poem to you.'

'Would you mourn for me?'

'Certainly,' I sighed.

'For a long time?'

'That depends.'

'On what?'

'The poem's excellence,' I replied.

IRVING LAYTON

Interview with a Poet

Are you a poet?
 Yes, I am.
How do you know?
 I've written poems.
If you've written poems it means you *were* a poet. But now?
 I'll write a poem again one day.
In that case maybe you'll be a poet again one day. But how will you know it is a poem?
 It will be a poem just like the last one.
Then of course it won't be a poem. A poem is only once and can never be the same a second time.
 I believe it will be just as good.
How can you be sure? Even the quality of a poem is for once only and depends not on you but on circumstances.
 I believe that circumstances will be the same too.
If you believe that then you won't be a poet and never were a poet. What then makes you think you are a poet?
 Well – I don't rightly know. And who are you?

MIROSLAV HOLUB
(translated by Ewald Osers)

CONVERSATIONS

Youth, Age and Poetry: A Dialogue

'What right have you to judge my poems, old man!'
He cried, eyes scintillant with youth and rage,
'I write in my heart's blood! I am sincere!
I speak the truth about my pain and passion,
Such torment you've forgotten at your age.'
The old man smiled. 'That's neither here nor there.'

'Poetry,' the boy exclaimed, 'unfolds like leaves.
Keats said it and you must admit he knew.
Its factory is the heart and not the head,
The intellect invariably deceives,
A lyric is as innocent as dew!'
'Keats didn't mean quite that,' the old man said.

'What was his meaning then? I'd like to hear!'
The old man spoke: 'The poem's seed will never
Be explained, but Keats well knew that true
Art is always wrought with skill and care,
That poets must be slippery and clever:
That's what I think he knew, or think I do.'

VERNON SCANNELL

In the East

Why are you moving your lips, said the Emperor I Tsung.

I am blessing the prophets, said Ibn Wahab the traveller.

Where are the prophets, said the Emperor I Tsung.
   I do not see them.

You see them, said Ibn Wahab the traveller:
   you do not recognize them but you see them.

I see a man in a boat on a great ocean, said the Emperor
     I Tsung.

That, said Ibn Wahab the traveller, is Noah,
   who swam on the world when the Flood drowned it.

I see a man in the fields, said the Emperor I Tsung:
   he is wandering.

That is Abraham, said Ibn Wahab the traveller:
   he is wandering everywhere looking for God.

I see a man on a tree, said the Emperor I Tsung.

That, said Ibn Wahab the traveller, is Jesus.

What did he do, said the Emperor I Tsung:
   did he swim on the world? Did he wander everywhere?

He died, said Ibn Wahab the traveller.

Why do I weep, said the Emperor I Tsung.

You have recognized Jesus, said Ibn Wahab the traveller.

                              ARCHIBALD MACLEISH

Vermont Conversation

'Good weather for hay.'
   'Yes, 'tis.'
'Mighty bright day.'
   'That's true.'
'Crops comin' on?'
   'Yep. You?'
'Tol'rable; beans got the blight.'
   'Way o' the Lord.'
'That's right.'

PATRICIA HUBBELL

Studup

'Owayer?'
'Imokay.'
'Gladtwearit.'
'Howbowchew?'
'Reelygrate.'
'Binwaytinlong?'
'Longinuff.'
'Owlongubinear?'
'Boutanour.'
'Thinkeelturnup?'
'Aventaclue.'
'Dewfancyim?'
'Sortalykim.'
'Wantadrinkorsummat?'
'Thanksilestayabit.'
'Soocherself.'
'Seeyalater.'
'Byfernow.'

BARRIE WADE

Daydreamer

'Aljenard, Winston, Frederick,
Spencer, wha ya look out the winda sa?'
'Me alook pun the nice green grass!'
'But why do you look apun the nice green grass?'
'Me na no!'

'Aljenard, Winston, Frederick Spencer,
wha are ya look out the winda sa?'
'Me alook pun the bright blue sky!'
'But why do you look apun the bright blue sky?'
'Me na no!'

'Aljenard, Winston, Frederick,
Spencer, what are ya look out the winda sa?'
'Me alook pun the hummin burd!'
'But why do you look apun the hummin burd?'
'Me na no!'

'Aljenard, Winston, Frederick,
Spencer, what are you look out the winda sa?'
'Me alook apun the glistening sun!'
'But why you look apun the glistening sun?'
'Me na no!'

'Aljenard, Winston, Frederick,
Spencer, wha are you look out the winda sa?'
'Me a try to feel the nice warm eir!'
'But why do you try to feel the nice warm eir?'

'Cause me a daydreamer!'

DAVID DURHAM

The Traveller

Old man, old man, sitting on the stile,
Your boots are worn, your clothes are torn,
   Tell us why you smile.

Children, children, what silly things you are!
My boots are worn and my clothes are torn
   Because I've walked so far.

Old man, old man, where have you walked from?
Your legs are bent, your breath is spent –
   Which way did you come?

Children, children, when you're old and lame,
When your legs are bent and your breath is spent
   You'll know the way I came.

Old man, old man, have you far to go
Without a friend to your journey's end,
   And why are you so slow?

Children, children, I do the best I may:
I meet a friend at my journey's end
   With whom you'll meet some day.

Old man, old man, sitting on the stile,
How do you know which way to go,
   And why is it you smile?

Children, children, butter should be spread,
Floors should be swept and promises kept –
   And you should be in bed!

RAYMOND WILSON

Talk to the Animals

Dialogue Between My Cat Bridget and Me

K: Can't you see
   I'm trying to write?
   Why jump on my knee?
   And why alight
   With muddy paws
   On verse brand-new?
   There should be laws
   Against cats like you.

B: *Can't you see*
   I'm writing too,
   Poems better
   Than you can do?

K: Is that a fact?
   We'll see about that.
   I must be cracked
   To put up with a cat
   That lies there dribbling
   And trying to bite a
   Bit off the ribbon
   Of my typewriter.

B: *I have to use*
   My tongue to say
   The words I want,
   Like you. OK?

K: Maybe so,
   But I don't see how.
   All you know
   To speak's *miaow*.

B: Different *miaows*.
   Sometimes I yell them,
   Sometimes whisper:
   It's the way I tell them.

K: You think you're a better
   Poet than me?

B: *So* that's *what you're*
   Supposed to be!

KIT WRIGHT

Cows

Half the time they munched the grass, and all the time
 they lay
Down in the water-meadows, the lazy month of May,
 A-chewing,
 A-mooing,
 To pass the hours away.

 'Nice weather,' said the brown cow.
 'Ah,' said the white.
 'Grass is very tasty.'
 'Grass is all right.'

Half the time they munched the grass, and all the time
 they lay
Down in the water-meadows, the lazy month of May,
 A-chewing,
 A-mooing,
 To pass the hours away.

 'Rain coming,' said the brown cow.
 'Ah,' said the white.
 'Flies is very tiresome.'
 'Flies bite.'

Half the time they munched the grass, and all the time
 they lay
Down in the water-meadows, the lazy month of May,
 A-chewing,
 A-mooing,
 To pass the hours away.

'Time to go,' said the brown cow.
    'Ah,' said the white.
  'Nice chat.' 'Very pleasant.'
    'Night.' 'Night.'

Half the time they munched the grass, and all the time they lay
Down in the water-meadows, the lazy month of May,
    A-chewing,
    A-mooing,
  To pass the hours away.

JAMES REEVES

Little Piggy

Where are you going, you little pig?
I'm leaving my mother, I'm growing so big!
   So big, young pig!
   So young, so big!
What, leaving your mother, you foolish young pig?

Where are you going, you little pig?
I've got a new spade, and I'm going to dig!
   To dig, little pig!
   A little pig dig!
Well, I never saw a pig with a spade that could dig!

Where are you going, you little pig?
Why, I'm going to have a nice ride in a gig!
   In a gig, little pig!
   What, a pig in a gig!
Well, I never yet saw a pig in a gig!

Where are you going, you little pig?
I'm going to the barber's to buy me a wig!
   A wig, little pig!
   A pig in a wig!
Why, whoever before saw a pig in a wig!

Where are you going, you little pig?
Why, I'm going to the ball to dance a fine jig!
   A jig, little pig!
   A pig dance a jig!
Well, I never before saw a pig dance a jig!

THOMAS HOOD

On a Night of Snow

Cat, if you go out-doors you must walk in the snow.
You will come back with little white shoes on your feet,
Little white slippers of snow that have heels of sleet.
Stay by the fire, my Cat. Lie still, do not go.
See how the flames are leaping and hissing low,
I will bring you a saucer of milk like a marguerite,
So white and so smooth, so spherical and so sweet –
Stay with me, Cat. Out-doors the wild winds blow.

Out-doors the wild winds blow, Mistress, and dark is the night.
Strange voices cry in the trees, intoning strange lore,
And more than cats move, lit by our eyes' green light,
On silent feet where the meadow grasses hang hoar –
Mistress, there are portents abroad of magic and might,
And things that are yet to be done. Open the door!

ELIZABETH COATSWORTH

This and That

Two cats together
In bee-heavy weather
After the August day
In smug contentment lay
By the garden shed
In the flower bed
Yawning out the hours
In the shade of the flowers
And passed the time away,

Between stretching and washing and sleeping,
Talking over the day.

'Climbed a tree.'
'Aaaah.'
'Terrorized sparrows.'
'Mmmmh.'
'Was chased.'
'Aaaah.'
'Fawned somewhat!'
'Mmmmh.'
'Washed, this and that,'
Said the first cat.

And they passed the time away
Between stretching and washing and sleeping
Talking over the day.

'Gazed out of parlour window.'
'Aaaah.'
'Pursued blue bottles.'
'Mmmmh.'
'Clawed curtains.'
'Aaaah.'
'Was cuffed.'
'Mmmmh.'
'Washed, this and that.'
Said the other cat.

And they passed the time away
Between stretching and washing and sleeping
Talking over the day.

'Scratched to be let in.'
'Aaaah.'
'Patrolled the house.'
'Mmmmh.'
'Scratched to go out.'
'Aaaah.'
'Was booted.'
'Mmmmh.'
'Washed, this and that.'
Said the first cat.

And they passed the time away
Between stretching and washing and sleeping
Talking over the day.

'Lapped cream elegantly.'
'Aaaah.'
'Disdained dinner.'
'Mmmmh.'
'Borrowed a little salmon.'
'Aaaah.'
'Was tormented.'
'Mmmmh.'
'Washed, this and that.'
Said the other cat.

And they passed the time away
Between stretching and washing and sleeping
Talking over the day.

GARETH OWEN

To My Dog Brock

'Brocklebank Flycatcher,
Why do you curse,
Hurling abuse at the dogs as they pass?'
'They are out. I am in. So I'll break through the glass.'

'Brocklebank Leashbreaker,
Why do you gnaw
Through your lead, hanging loose, as you sit in the car?'
'It irks me. It jerks me. I need to run far.'

'Brocklebank Armbiter,
Why do you grasp
My wrist when I'm back, knock me down, hold me fast?'
'I hurt you for joy that you've come home at last.'

'Brocklebank Thigh-hugger,
Why do you furl,
Pressed hard up against me, curled round in a ball?'
'It is warm. It is womb. It is us. It is all.'

DAVID KING

It Is I, the Little Owl

Who is it up there on top of the lodge?
Who is it up there on top of the lodge?
  It is I,
  The little owl,
  coming down –
  It is I,
  The little owl,
  coming down –
  coming down –
  down –
  coming
  down –
  down –

Who is it whose eyes are shining up there?
Who is it whose eyes are shining up there?
  It is I,
  The little owl,
  coming down –
  It is I,
  The little owl,
  coming down –
  coming –
  down –
  coming
  down –
  down –

                                          CHIPPEWA INDIAN

Raccoon

One summer night a little Raccoon,
Above his left shoulder, looked at the new moon.
    He made a wish;
    He said: 'I wish
    I were a Catfish,
    A Blowfish, a Squid,
    A Katydid,
    A Beetle, a Skink,
    An Ostrich, a pink
    Flamingo, a Gander,
    A Salamander,
    A Hippopotamus,
    A Duck-billed Platypus,
    A Gecko, a Slug,
    A Water Bug,
    A pug-nosed Beaver,
    Anything whatever
Except what I am, a little Raccoon!'

Above his left shoulder, the Evening Star
Listened and heard the little Raccoon
    Who wished on the moon;
    And she said: 'Why wish
    You were a Catfish,
    A Blowfish, a Squid,
    A Katydid,
    A Beetle, a Skink,
    An Ostrich, a pink
    Flamingo, a Gander,
    A Salamander,
    A Hippopotamus,
    A Duck-billed Platypus,
    A Gecko, a Slug,
    A Water Bug,
    A pug-nosed Beaver,
    Anything whatever?
Why must you change?' said the Evening Star,
'When you are perfect as you are?
I know a boy who wished on the moon
That *he* might be a little Raccoon!'

                                          WILLIAM JAY SMITH

The Tickle Rhyme

'Who's that tickling my back?' said the wall.
'Me,' said a small
Caterpillar. 'I'm learning
To crawl.'

IAN SERRAILLIER

The Flamingo

FIRST VOICE

Oh! tell me have you ever seen a red long-leg'd
                                    Flamingo?
Oh! tell me have you ever seen him the water in go?

SECOND VOICE

Oh! yes at Bowling-Green I've seen a red, long-leg'd
                                    Flamingo,
Oh! yes at Bowling-Green I've there seen him the water
                                        in go.

FIRST VOICE

Oh! tell me did you ever see a bird so funny stand-o
When forth he from the water comes and gets upon the
                                      land-o?

SECOND VOICE

No! in my life I ne'er did see a bird so funny stand-o
When forth he from the water comes and gets upon the
                                      land-o.

FIRST VOICE
He has a leg some three feet long, or near it, so they
                                                          say, Sir.
Stiff upon one alone he stands, t'other he stows away, Sir.

SECOND VOICE
And what an ugly head he's got! I wonder that he'd
                                                          wear it.
But rather *more* I wonder that his long, thin neck can
                                                          bear it.

FIRST VOICE
And think, this length of neck and legs (no doubt they
                                                    have their uses)
Are members of a little frame, much smaller than a
                                                         goose's!

SECOND VOICE
Oh! isn't he a curious bird, that red, long-leg'd Flamingo?
A water bird, a gawky bird, a singular bird, by jingo!

LEWIS GAYLORD CLARK

David and Goliath

With lazy humming flight
Aggression enters the kitchen,
Alights on the table,
A yellow and black abdomen taps the cloth.

'Shoo, you've no business here.'
'September grows cold, let me in.'
'Out! Out, where you belong.'
'You have stored the summer in jars,
Let me in.'

We argue the point he and I.
I slowly fold a newspaper.
He, lifts off.
I retreat into the garden.

CATHERINE BENSON

Catching a Carp

      ANGLER
Fish, come-come, waddle-come,
Sway your fat copper sides.
Flip-flip your fins, little one,
Where my line guides.

                        FISH
               Green water cool to breathe,
               Green mud, green beds of reeds.

      ANGLER
Fish, move now, move to me,
Stream to my hook.
Fish, run the pebble rills,
Gulp gills. Fish look!

                        FISH
               Oo. Red bug is dancing there,
               Dropped from the silver air.

      ANGLER
Hush, heart, hush, fish will hear
Drumbangs – and disappear . . .

                        FISH
               I come-come, waddle-come,
               Sway my fat copper sides.
               Aiming for you, sugar-bug,
               Soon down my throat you will slide.

        ANGLER
Sidling up close like a ghost
Shadowy under the shine . . .

                          FISH
            What is that light, thin and straight?
            What is that? . . . Line?

          BOTH TOGETHER
    Ah well, another day, next time we meet
           I will discover if

    ANGLER   **FISH**
     fish   bugs

        BOTH TOGETHER
          taste sweet.

                                JAN DEAN

The Barn

'I am tired of this barn!' said the colt.
'And every day it snows.
Outside there's no grass any more
And icicles grow on my nose.
I am tired of hearing the cows
Breathing and talking together.
I am sick of these clucking hens.
I *hate* stables and winter weather!'

'Hush, little colt,' said the mare.
'And a story I will tell
Of a barn like this one of ours
And the wonders that there befell.
It was weather much like this,
And the beasts stood as we stand now
In the warm good dark of the barn –
A horse and an ass and a cow.'

'And sheep?' asked the colt. 'Yes, sheep,
And a pig and a goat and a hen.
All of the beasts of the barnyard,
The usual servants of men.
And into their midst came a lady
And she was cold as death,
But the animals leaned above her
And made her warm with their breath.

There was her baby born
And laid to sleep in the hay,
While music flooded the rafters
And the barn was as light as day.
And angels and kings and shepherds
Came to worship the babe from afar,
But we looked at him first of all creatures
By the bright strange light of a star!'

ELIZABETH COATSWORTH

'I', Said the Donkey

'I,' said the donkey, all shaggy and brown,
'Carried his mother all into the town,
Carried her uphill, carried her down.
I,' said the donkey, all shaggy and brown.

'I,' said the cow, with spots of red,
'Gave him hay for to rest his head,
Gave a manger for his bed.
I,' said the cow, with spots of red.

'I,' said the sheep, with twisted horn,
'Gave my wool for to keep him warm,
Gave my coat on Christmas morn.
I,' said the sheep with twisted horn.

'I,' said the dove from the rafters high,
'Cooed him to sleep with a lullaby,
Cooed him to sleep my mate and I.
I,' said the dove from the rafters high.

ANON

Noah and the Rabbit

'No land,' said Noah,
'There – is – not – any – land.
Oh, Rabbit, Rabbit, can't you understand?'

But Rabbit shook his head:
'Say it again,' he said:
'And slowly, please.
No good brown earth for burrows,
And no trees;
No wastes where vetch and rabbit-parsley grows,
No brakes, no bushes and no turnip rows,
No holt, no upland, meadowland or weald,
No tangled hedgerow and no playtime field?'

'No land at all – just water,' Noah replied,
And Rabbit sighed.
'For always, Noah?' he whispered, 'will there be
Nothing henceforth for ever but the sea?
Or will there come a day
When the green earth will call me back to play?'

Noah bowed his head:
'Some day . . . some day,' he said.

HUGH CHESTERMAN

A Footprint on the Air

'Stay!' said the child. The bird said, 'No,
My wing has mended, I must go.
I shall come back to see you though,
One night, one day – '
                      'How shall I know?'
'Look for my footprint in the snow.'

'The snow soon goes – oh, that's not fair!'
'Don't grieve. Don't grieve. I shall be there
In the bright season of the year,
One night, one day – '
                      'But tell me, where?'
'Look for my footprint on the air.'

NAOMI LEWIS

Ghostly Gossip

Green Candles

'There's someone at the door,' said gold candlestick:
'Let her in quick. Let her in quick!'
'There is a small hand groping at the handle:
Why don't you turn it?' asked green candle.

'Don't go, don't go,' said the Hepplewhite chair,
'Lest you find a strange lady there.'
'Yes, stay where you are,' whispered the white wall:
'There is nobody there at all.'

'I know her little foot,' grey carpet said:
'Who but I should know her light tread?'
'She shall come in,' answered the open door,
'And not,' said the room, 'go out any more.'

HUMBERT WOLFE

Who's in the Next Room?

'Who's in the next room? – who?
    I seemed to see
Somebody in the dawning passing through,
    Unknown to me.'
'Nay: you saw nought. He passed invisibly.'

'Who's in the next room? – who?
    I seem to hear
Somebody muttering firm in a language new
    That chills the ear.'
'No: you catch not his tongue who has entered there.'

'Who's in the next room? – who?
    I seem to feel
His breath like a clammy draught, as if it drew
    From the Polar Wheel.'
'No: none who breathes at all does the door conceal.'

'Who's in the next room? – who?
    A figure wan
With a message to one in there of something due?
    Shall I know him anon?'
'Yea he; and he brought such; and you'll know him anon.'

THOMAS HARDY

Johnny Dow

    Wha lies here?
I, Johnny Dow.
    Hoo! Johnny is that you?
Ay, man, but a'm dead now.

ANON

Bones

Said Mr Smith, 'I really cannot
    Tell you, Dr Jones –
The most peculiar pain I'm in –
    I think it's in my *bones*.'

Said Dr Jones, 'Oh, Mr Smith,
    That's nothing. Without doubt
We have a simple cure for that;
    It is to take them out.'

He laid forthwith poor Mr Smith
    Close-clamped upon the table,
And, cold as stone, took out his bones
    As fast as he was able.

And Smith said, 'Thank you, thank you, *thank* you,'
    And wished him a Good-day;
And with his parcel 'neath his arm
    He slowly moved away.

WALTER DE LA MARE

Grave Talk

As I walked down the churchyard
   I heard a dead man say,
'Is that my old friend, Stephen,
   That's passing by this way?'

Now you might think a dead man's voice
   Would fill the heart with dread,
But if Tom never hurt me, living,
   What harm should he do me, dead?

'Ay, Tom, it's Stephen, right enough.
   I keep your memory green,
For it's many a time I've missed you
   Since you died last Hallowe'en!'

'Ah, if only you knew how often
   I've summoned you, as you've passed;
But now you hear me, rest assured
   All will be well at last!'

'But how is it I can hear you now,
   When I never heard you before?'
'Friend Stephen, there are mysteries
   You'd do better to ignore!'

'But tell me – how and where you are?
  And do you rot in clay?
Or are you fed, and clothed and shod
  In a far brighter day?'

'Spare me your questions, Stephen, then I
  Need tell you no lies!'
'But are you in Purgatory or Hell,
  Or perhaps Paradise?'

'Hush and be patient, my good old friend! –
  The mysteries you would know
Will be yours to keep for ever
  By tomorrow's cock-crow!'

RAYMOND WILSON

Ghosts

That's right. Sit down and talk to me.
What do you want to talk about?

Ghosts. You were saying that you believe in them.
Yes, they exist, without a doubt.

What, bony white nightmares that rattle and glow?
No, just spirits that come and go.

I've never heard such a load of rubbish.
Never mind, one day you'll know.

What makes you so sure?

I said:
What makes you so sure?

Hey,
Where did you go?

KIT WRIGHT

We Are Seven

I met a little cottage Girl:
She was eight years old, she said;
Her hair was thick with many a curl
That clustered round her head.

She had a rustic, woodland air,
And she was wildly clad:
Her eyes were fair, and very fair;
– Her beauty made me glad.

'Sisters and brothers, little Maid,
How many may you be?'
'How many? Seven in all,' she said
And wondering looked at me.

'And where are they? I pray you tell.'
She answered, 'Seven are we;
And two of us at Conway dwell.
And two are gone to sea.

Two of us in the church-yard lie,
My sister and my brother;
And, in the church-yard cottage, I
Dwell near them with my mother.'

'You say that two at Conway dwell,
And two are gone to sea,
Yet ye are seven! – I pray you tell,
Sweet Maid, how this may be.'

Then did the little Maid reply,
'Seven boys and girls are we;
Two of us in the church-yard lie,
Beneath the church-yard tree.'

'You run about, my little Maid,
Your limbs they are alive;
If two are in the church-yard laid,
Then ye are only five.'

'Their graves are green they may be seen,'
The little Maid replied.
'Twelve steps or more from my mother's door,
And they are side by side.

My stockings there I often knit,
My kerchief there I hem;
And there upon the ground I sit,
And sing a song to them.

And often after sunset, Sir,
When it is light and fair,
I take my little porringer,
And eat my supper there.

The first that died was sister Jane;
In bed she moaning lay,
Till God released her of her pain;
And then she went away.

So in the church-yard she was laid;
And, when the grass was dry,
Together round her grave we played,
My brother John and I.

And when the ground was white with snow,
And I could run and slide,
My brother John was forced to go,
And he lies by her side.'

'How many are you, then,' said I,
'If they two are in heaven?'
Quick was the little Maid's reply,
'O Master! we are seven.'

'But they are dead; those two are dead!
Their spirits are in heaven!'
'Twas throwing words away; for still
The little Maid would have her will,
And said, 'Nay, we are seven!'

WILLIAM WORDSWORTH

Unwelcome Guest

Mr Weggs lived with Mrs Weggs,
Just Mrs Weggs and he.
They lived alone with their two selves
As happily as could be,
Until one night, they found with a fright
They were washing up for three!

'It can't be a mouse,' said Mrs Weggs,
'A mouse does not drink tea.
There's no one at all, from roof to hall,
Except for you and me.
Yet as sure, Mr Weggs, as eggs is eggs,
We're washing up for three!'

'It must be a ghost,' said Mr Weggs,
'A ghost we cannot see.
Without so much as "By your leave",
A "please" or "pardon me".
It sits on a chair that isn't there
And scrummages our tea!'

'I don't like uninvited ghosts
Who come without a key;
We must give him notice, Mr Weggs,
And from today,' said she.
'We'll write to the ghost by the very next post –
The door-post it must be: –

'*"Dear Mr Ghost, we're glad you called,*
But both of us agree
You'd be better off at Mr Brown's
Which overlooks the sea.
Besides, one only, he's rather lonely,
And needs you more than we."'

'He's gone,' said Mr Weggs next night.
'He's gone – the house is free.'
'Ah good, Mr Weggs,' said Mrs Weggs.
'It's such a relief to see
No extra cup when one's washing up –
Two's company, not three!'

CLIVE SANSOM

A Frosty Night

'Alice, dear, what ails you,
   Dazed and lost and shaken?
Has the chill night numbed you?
   Is it fright you have taken?'

'Mother, I am very well,
   I was never better.
Mother, do not hold me so,
   Let me write my letter.'

'Sweet, my dear, what ails you?'
　'No, but I am well.
The night was cold and frosty –
　There's no more to tell.'

'Ay, the night was frosty,
　Coldly gaped the moon,
Yet the birds seemed twittering
　Through green boughs of June.

Soft and thick the snow lay,
　Stars danced in the sky –
Not all the lambs of May-day
　Skip so bold and high.

Your feet were dancing, Alice,
　Seemed to dance on air,
You looked a ghost or angel
　In the star-light there.

Your eyes were frosted star-light;
　Your heart, fire and snow.
Who was it said, "I love you"?'
　'Mother, let me go!'

ROBERT GRAVES

from *Little Mary Crosbie*

Some little children from the village discuss
'That one as has come to Winter's for a bit.'
'I saw her on Monday when I fetched the washing,
She gave me a pansy off Mrs Winter's garden,
And we played jumping off them garden steps.
She calls yon steps by names she's made for 'em.'
'She's out of a Home.' 'Who told you?' 'I knowed it meself.
I saw them fetch her.' 'She says she's going to stop.'
'Will she be coming to school?' 'Of course she will.
She's been at school afore. She's going to show me
Her house, she says.' 'Where's that?' 'Across the way.'

'Oh, folks says that's a house with dobbies in.'
'She goes to play there.' 'She'll be mates with dobbies.
Her hair's like that.' 'What?' 'Like as if she'd seen one,
All stood on end.' 'Next time I'm going to ask her
About them dobbies, if she's ever seen one.'
'She showed me a bird nest Mrs Winter showed her,
When I was by, I took an egg, and dropped it;
She like as if she might have hit me for it,
So I ran off.' 'Well, I shall go again,
I like jumping off steps with funny names.'

MARGARET CROPPER

Her-zie

A troll and his wife speak of the human child they stole.

What's wrong with you-zie?
Nothing with me-zie,
Then what with who-zie?
Only with Her-zie,
So what with Her-zie?
A hearse for her-zie
A hearse for her-zie
Came for her.

What colour was it then?
Golden, golden,
Was there anyone in it?
A pale king was in it.
That was not a hearse for Her-zie, husband,
It was her marriage carriage.
It was a hearse for me, then,
My heart went with them and died then.

Husband, ah me-zie,
Your heart has died for Her-zie,
Without it you cannot be easy.

STEVIE SMITH

Overheard on a Saltmarsh

Nymph, nymph, what are your beads?
Green glass, goblin. Why do you stare at them?
Give them me.

           No.
Give them me. Give them me.
           No.
Then I will howl all night in the reeds,
Lie in the mud and howl for them.

Goblin, why do you love them so?

They are better than stars or water,
Better than voices of winds that sing,
Better than any man's fair daughter,
Your green glass beads on a silver ring.

Hush I stole them out of the moon.

Give me your beads, I desire them.
           No.
I will howl in a deep lagoon
For your green glass beads, I love them so.
Give them me. Give them.
           No.

                              HAROLD MONRO

The Two Rivers

Said Tweed to Till
'What gars ye rin sae still?'
Said Till to Tweed
'Though ye rin wi' speed
And I rin slaw,
For every man that ye droon
I droon twa.'

ANON

Gargoyles

Crouch we and leer from our quoin* of the guttering,
And rain in our jowls goes a-gurgling and spluttering.

'Splodge be my name!' – 'Splurge be mine!' –
Thus we squat, come foul, come fine.

Drought in the city, drought on the plain:
Dry lips gaping, we thirst for rain.

'Splurge, be watching?' – 'Splodge, be hearkening?' –
'Thunder are rolling' – 'Clouds do be darkening.'

First but a licking, a spittling, a tickling,
Then on to our gums the rain comes trickling.

* quoin – corner-stone

'Splodge, be gladsome?' – 'Ay, that I be:
Sky-water, Splurge, be the dose for we!'

Down they roof and along them spout,
Sliding and streaming it oozes out.

Hark on the leads to the pitter-patter
Where a million cloud-drops spill and spatter!

And as on our backs the floods be a-dashing,
Our mouth-jets into the earth go splashing.

'Storm do be heavier!' – 'Stream do be stronger!' –
Our chops get fuller and our squirt gets longer!

And ah, what joy! and oh, what wonder!
To spit on the church-men scattering under!

Dean and canons go scampering by,
Sheltering pates from the leaking sky;

But Splodge and Splurge have nought to fear –
High hob-goblins what hob-nob here!

CLIVE SANSOM

Hallowe'en

'Granny, I saw a witch go by,
I saw two, I saw three!
I heard their skirts go swish, swish, swish – '

   'Child, 'twas leaves against the sky,
   And the autumn wind in the tree.'

'Granny, broomsticks they bestrode,
Their hats were black as tar,
And buckles twinkled on their shoes – '

   'You saw but shadows on the road,
   The sparkle of a star.'

'Granny, all their heels were red,
Their cats were big as sheep.
I heard a bat say to an owl – '

   'Child, you must go straight to bed,
   'Tis time you were asleep.'

'Granny, I saw men in green
Their eyes shone fiery red,
Their heads were yellow pumpkins – '

   'Now you've told me what you've seen,
   WILL you go to bed?'

'Granny?'

  'Well?'

'Don't you believe – ?'

  'What?'

'What I've seen?
Don't you know it's Hallowe'en?'

MARIE A. LAWSON

Witch, Witch

'Witch, witch, where do you fly?' . . .
'Under the clouds and over the sky.'

'Witch, witch, what do you eat?' . . .
'Little black apples from Hurricane Street.'

'Witch, witch, what do you drink?' . . .
'Vinegar, blacking, and good red ink.'

'Witch, witch, where do you sleep?' . . .
'Up in the clouds where pillows are cheap.'

ROSE FYLEMAN

The Witches, from *Macbeth*

FIRST WITCH
Round about the cauldron go;
In the poison'd entrails throw.
Toad, that under cold stone
Days and night has thirty-one
Swelter'd venom sleeping got,
Boil thou first i' the charmed pot.

ALL
Double, double toil and trouble;
Fire, burn; and cauldron, bubble.

SECOND WITCH
Fillet of a fenny snake,
In the cauldron boil and bake;
Eye of newt, and toe of frog,
Wool of bat, and tongue of dog,
Adder's fork and blind-worm's sting,
Lizard's leg, and howlet's wing,
For a charm of powerful trouble,
Like a hell-broth boil and bubble.

ALL
Double, double toil and trouble;
Fire, burn; and cauldron, bubble.

THIRD WITCH
Scale of dragon, tooth of wolf,
Witches' mummy, maw and gulf
Of the ravin'd salt-sea shark,
Root of hemlock digg'd i' the dark . . .
. . . Add thereto a tiger's chaudron,
For th' ingredients of our cauldron.

ALL
Double, double toil and trouble;
Fire, burn; and cauldron, bubble.

SECOND WITCH
Cool it with a baboon's blood,
Then the charm is firm and good . . .
By the pricking of my thumbs,
Something wicked this way comes:
    Open, locks,
    Whoever knocks!

MACBETH
How now, you secret, black, and midnight hags!
What is't you do?

ALL
A deed without a name.

WILLIAM SHAKESPEARE

GHOSTLY GOSSIP

Let Us In

'Let us in! Let us in!'
Who is crying above the wind's din?

'Let us in! Let us in!
We are pale and cold and thin.'

A clock chimes the midnight hour.
Are they creatures with magic power?

'Let us in! Let us in!
We are pale and cold and thin.'

They come and come and more and more.
Close the curtains! Lock the door!

'Let us in! Let us in!
We are pale and cold and thin.'

'Let us in! Let us in!
We are pale and cold and thin.'

OLIVE DOVE

The Night Express

   Who heard a whistle in the night, so far,
   Who heard the whistle of the train pass?
– I heard,
   Said a hedge-safe bird,
– And I, said the bleached grass.
– I heard, said the sinking star,
– And I, said the apple, nested on the ground,
– And I, the mooned church-tower said,
– And I, the graves around.
– And you, said the roof of the farm overhead
   To the child in bed,
   You heard the sound.
– I, said the child, asleep almost,
   I heard it plain,
   I heard the whistle, the whistle of the train,
   Like a friend, like a ghost.

                                          FRANCES CORNFORD

Imagine That

The Toys Talk of the World

'I should like,' said the vase from the china-store,
'To have seen the world a little more.

When they carried me here I was wrapped up tight,
But they say it is really a lovely sight.'

'Yes,' said a little plaster bird,
'That is exactly what *I* have heard;

There are thousands of trees, and oh, what a sight
It must be when the candles are all alight.'

The fat top rolled on his other side:
'It is not in the least like that,' he cried.

'Except myself and the kite and ball,
None of you know the world at all.

There are houses, and pavements hard and red,
And everything spins around,' he said;

'Sometimes it goes slowly, and sometimes fast,
And often it stops with a bump at last.'

The wooden donkey nodded his head:
'I had heard the world was like that,' he said.

The kite and the ball exchanged a smile,
But they did not speak; it was not worth while.

KATHARINE PYLE

The Table and the Chair

I

Said the Table to the Chair,
'You can hardly be aware,
How I suffer from the heat,
And from chilblains on my feet!
If we took a little walk,
We might have a little talk!
Pray let us take the air!'
Said the Table to the Chair.

II

Said the Chair unto the Table,
'Now you *know* we are not able!
How foolishly you talk,
When you know we *cannot* walk!'
Said the Table, with a sigh,
'It can do no harm to try,
I've as many legs as you,
Why can't we walk on two?'

III

So they both went slowly down,
And walked about the town
With a cheerful bumpy sound,
As they toddled round and round.
And everybody cried,
As they hastened to their side,
'See! the Table and the Chair
Have come out to take the air!'

IV

But in going down an alley,
To a castle in a valley,
They completely lost their way,
And wandered all the day,
Till, to see them safely back,
They paid a Ducky-quack,
And a Beetle, and a Mouse,
Who took them to their house.

V

Then they whispered to each other,
'O delightful little brother!
What a lovely walk we've taken!
Let us dine on Beans and Bacon!'
So the Ducky, and the leetle
Browny-Mousy and the Beetle
Dined, and danced upon their heads
Till they toddled to their beds.

EDWARD LEAR

The Lady of Shalots

'Have you forgotten, Curly Head,
That night beside the Parsley Bed?'
'I have forgotten it,' she said.

'Do you recall the word you spoke
That night beneath the Artichoke?'
'Oh, that,' said she, 'was just a joke.'

'Have you forgotten how you cried
Among the Onions?' I sighed.
'Well, do you blame me?' she replied.

I spoke of sympathetic scenes
Between the Parsnips and the Beans;
But when I called her my Shalot
And said what Celery I got –
She told me not to talk such rot.

Ah, Kitchen Garden, soaked in rain
I ne'er shall see her like again.

REGINALD ARKELL

IMAGINE THAT

Jam

'Spread,' said Toast to Butter,
And Butter spread.
'That's better, Butter,'
Toast said.

'Jam,' said Butter to Toast.
'Where are you, Jam,
When we need you most?'
Jam: 'Here I am,

Strawberry, trickly and sweet.
How are you, Spoon?'
'I'm helping somebody eat,
I think, pretty soon.'

DAVID MCCORD

Cross Purposes

A knight am I so bold and brave;
    Yes, yes. *She.* No, no.
And you the damsel I must save;
    Yes, yes. *She.* No, no.

She. 'Tis I am Mab, the fairy queen;
    Yes, yes. *He.* No, no.
She. I'll pinch you till you're blue and green;
    Yes, yes. *He.* No, no.

He. A mighty wingèd Jinn am I;
    Yes, yes. *She.* No, no.
He. Away, away with you I'll fly;
    Yes, yes. *She.* No, no.

She. I'll be a fair enchanting ghoul;
    Yes, yes. *He.* No, no.
She. And you I'll change into a mule;
    Yes, yes. *He.* No, no.

Both. What can we do will please the two?
    Ah ah! Oh, oh!
  Why I'll be I and you'll be you;
    Ha, ha! ho, ho!

MRS RICHARD STRACHEY

My True Love

On Monday, Monday,
  My True Love said to me,
'I've brought you this nice pumpkin;
  I picked it off a tree!'

On Tuesday, Tuesday,
  My True Love said to me,
'Look – I've brought you sand tarts;
  I got them by the sea.'

On Wednesday, Wednesday,
  My True Love said to me,
'I've caught you this white polar bear;
  It came from Tennessee.'

On Thursday, Thursday,
  My True Love said to me,
'This singing yellow butterfly
  I've all for you, from me.'

On Friday, Friday,
  My True Love said to me,
'Here's a long-tailed guinea pig;
  It's frisky as can be.'

On Saturday, Saturday,
  To my True Love I said,
'You have not told me ONE TRUE THING,
  So you I'll never wed!'

IVY O. EASTWICK

There Was a Lady Loved a Swine

There was a lady loved a swine.
'Honey!' said she;
'Pig-hog, wilt thou be mine?'
'Hunc!' said he.

'I'll build thee a silver sty,
Honey,' said she;
'And in it thou shalt lie!'
'Hunc!' said he.

'Pinned with a silver pin,
Honey,' said she;
'That thou mayest go out and in,'
'Hunc!' said he.

'Will thou have me now,
Honey,' said she;
'Speak, or my heart will break,'
'Hunc!' said he.

ANON

Lanky Lee and Lindy Lou

Said Lanky Lee
To Lindy Lou,
'Please let me run
Away with you!'
But Lou replied
With frustration:
'You've got no
Imagination,
For that is all,
Dear Lanky Lee,
That ever runs
Away with *me*!'

COLIN WEST

If I Were a Queen

'If I were a Queen,
 What would I do?
I'd make you King,
 And I'd wait on you.'

'If I were a King,
 What would I do?
I'd make you Queen,
 For I'd marry you.'

CHRISTINA ROSSETTI

IMAGINE THAT

The Flattered Flying-Fish

Said the Shark to the Flying-Fish over the phone:
'Will you join me tonight? I am dining alone.
Let me order a nice little dinner for two!
And come as you are, in your shimmering blue.'

Said the Flying-Fish: 'Fancy remembering me,
And the dress that I wore at the Porpoises' tea!'
'How could I forget?' said the Shark in his guile:
'I expect you at eight!' and rang off with a smile.

She has powdered her nose; she has put on her things;
She is off with one flap of her luminous wings.
O little one, lovely, light-hearted and vain,
The Moon will not shine on your beauty again!

E. V. RIEU

Johnny Sands

A man whose name was Johnny Sands
    Had married Betty Hague,
And though she brought him gold and lands
    She proved a terrible plague.
For, O, she was a scolding wife,
    Full of caprice and whim;
He said that he was tired of life,
    And she was tired of him.

Says he, 'Then I will drown myself;
   The river runs below.'
Says she, 'Pray do, you silly elf,
   I wished it long ago.'
Says he, 'Upon the brink I'll stand,
   Do you run down the hill
And push me in with all your might.'
   Says she, 'My love, I will.'

'For fear that I should courage lack,
   And try to save my life,
Pray tie my hands behind my back.'
   'I will,' replied his wife.
She tied them fast as you may think,
   And when securely done,
'Now stand,' says she, 'upon the brink
   And I'll prepare to run.'

All down the hill his loving bride
   Now ran with all her force
To push him in – he stepped aside,
   And she fell in, of course.
Now splashing, dashing like a fish,
   'O, save me, Johnny Sands!'
'I can't, my dear, though much I wish,
   For you have tied my hands!'

ANON

My Very Peculiar Pet

When I was young I used to think
I had a pet called Fred,
I was too young to understand
My pet was in my head.

I'd take him out for little walks
Around the block each day,
He'd always run ahead of me
Then in the park we'd play.

One day my mother said to me,
'Why do you talk this way?
I think I'll call the doctor round
Whatever will he say?'

I told the doctor what Fred ate,
Maggots, worms and flies,
I said my pet had horns and wings
And spots and big green eyes.

He told my mother, 'Do not fret
About her funny ways,
She's not as strange as she may seem
She's going through a phase.'

IMAGINE THAT

The doctor asked me last, not least,
'What is your pet, my child?'
'He is a dragon, sir,' I said,
The grown-ups only smiled.

I'm older now and understand,
There never was a Fred,
Don't worry that I'm lonely,
I've his brother George instead.

HANNAH MCBAIN

The First Men on Mercury

– We come in peace from the third planet.
Would you take us to your leader?

– Bawr stretter! Bawr. Bawr. Stretterhawl?

– This is a little plastic model
of the solar system, with working parts.
You are here and we are there and we
are now here with you, is this clear?

– Gawl horrop. Bawr. Abawrhannahanna!

– Where we come from is blue and white
with brown, you see we call the brown
here 'land', the blue is 'sea', and the white
is 'clouds' over land and sea, we live
on the surface of the brown land,
all round is sea and clouds. We are 'men'.
Men come –

– Glawp men! Gawrbenner menko. Menhawl?

– Men come in peace from the third planet
which we call 'earth'. We are earthmen.
Take us earthmen to your leader.

– Thmen? Thmen? Bawr. Bawrhossop.
Yuleeda tan hanna. Harrabost yuleeda.

– I am the yuleeda. You see my hands,
we carry not benner, we come in peace.
The spaceways are all stretterhawn.

– Glawn peacemen all horrabhanna tantko!
Tan come at'mstrossop. Glawp yuleeda!

– Atoms are peacegawl in our harraban.
Menbat worrabost from tan hannahanna.

– You men we know bawrhossoptant. Bawr.
We know yuleeda. Go strawg backspetter quick.

– We cantantabawr, tantingko backspetter now!

– Banghapper now! Yes, third planet back.
Yuleeda will go back blue, white, brown
nowhanna! There is no more talk.

– Gawl han fasthapper?

– No. You must go back to your planet.
Go back in peace, take what you have gained
but quickly.

– Stretterworra gawl, gawl . . .

– Of course, but nothing is ever the same,
now is it? You'll remember Mercury.

EDWIN MORGAN

How to Treat Elves

I met an elf-man in the woods,
    The weest little elf!
Sitting under a mushroom tall –
    'Twas taller than himself!

'How do you do, little elf?' I said,
    'And what do you do all day?'
'I dance 'n frolic about,' said he,
    ''N scuttle about and play;

I s'prise the butterflies, 'n when
    A katydid I see,
"Katy didn't!" I say, and he
    Says "Katy did!" to me!

I hide behind my mushroom stalk
    When Mister Mole comes froo,
'N only jus' to fwighten him
    I jump out 'n say "Boo!"

'N then I swing on a cobweb swing
    Up in the air so high,
'N the chicklets chirp to hear me sing
    "Upsy-daisy die!"

IMAGINE THAT

'N then I play with the baby chicks,
   I call them, chick chick chick!
'N what do you think of that?' said he.
   I said, 'It makes me sick.

It gives me sharp and shooting pains
   To listen to such drool.'
I lifted up my foot and squashed
   The God damn little fool.

MORRIS BISHOP

Some Curious Habits of Jonathan Bing

'Why do you sit by yourself in the sun,
   Jonathan Bing, Jonathan Bing?
Why do you sit by yourself in the sun,
When you know there is plenty of work to be done,
   Jonathan, Jonathan Bing?'

'Why, do you ask, by myself do I sit?'
   Said Jonathan Bing, Jonathan Bing,
'The question is foolish, as you must admit,
For there's no one, I think, that can *help* me to sit,'
   Said Jonathan, Jonathan Bing.

'Why do you sit on the floor, if you please,
   Jonathan Bing, Jonathan Bing?
Why do you sit on the floor, if you please,
Holding a dining room chair on your knees,
   Jonathan, Jonathan Bing?'

'For sixty-odd years, without any mishap,'
   Said Jonathan Bing, Jonathan Bing,
'This chair has supported my weight on its lap,
Now it's sitting on me while it takes a short nap,'
   Said Jonathan, Jonathan Bing.

'What are you making that racket about,
   Jonathan Bing, Jonathan Bing?
What are you chipping and chopping about,
Why are you taking that staircase out,
   Jonathan, Jonathan Bing?'

'I'm turning it up so it stands on its head,'
   Said Jonathan Bing, Jonathan Bing,
'So the stairs will go *down* when I go up to bed,
And if they go *up* when I come down, instead,
   What matter?' said Jonathan Bing.

                           BEATRICE CURTIS BROWN

IMAGINE THAT

You Can't Be That

I told them:
When I grow up
I'm not going to be a scientist
Or someone who reads the news on TV.
No, a million birds will fly through me.
I'M GOING TO BE A TREE!

They said,
You can't be that. No, you can't be that.

I told them:
When I grow up
I'm not going to be an airline pilot,
A dancer, a lawyer or an MC.
No, huge whales will swim in me.
I'M GOING TO BE AN OCEAN!

They said,
You can't be that. No, you can't be that.

I told them:
I'm not going to be a DJ,
A computer programmer, a musician or a beautician.
No, streams will flow through me, I'll be the home of eagles;
I'll be full of nooks, crannies, valleys and fountains.
I'M GOING TO BE A RANGE OF MOUNTAINS!

IMAGINE THAT

They said,
You can't be that. No, you can't be that.

I asked them:
Just what do you think I am?
Just a child, they said,
*And children always become
At least one of the things
We want them to be.*

They do not understand me.
I'll be a stable if I want, smelling of fresh hay,
I'll be a lost glade in which unicorns still play.
They do not realize I can fulfil
Any ambition.
They do not realize among them
Walks a magician.

BRIAN PATTEN

Storytime

Once upon a time, children,
there lived a fearsome dragon . . .

*Please, miss,
Jamie's made a dragon.
Out in the sandpit.*

Lovely, Andrew.
Now this dragon
had enormous red eyes
and a swirling, whirling tail . . .

*Jamie's dragon's got
yellow eyes, miss.*

Lovely, Andrew.
Now this dragon was
as wide as a horse
as green as the grass
as tall as a house . . .

*Jamie's would JUST fit
in our classroom, miss!*

But he was a very friendly dragon . . .

Jamie's dragon ISN'T, miss.
He eats people, miss.
Especially TEACHERS,
Jamie said.

Very nice, Andrew!

Now one day, children,
this enormous dragon
rolled his red eye,
whirled his swirly green tail
and set off to find . . .

His dinner, miss!
Because he was hungry, miss!

Thank you, Andrew.
He rolled his red eye,
whirled his green tail,
and opened his wide, wide mouth
until

Please, miss,
I did try to tell you, miss!

JUDITH NICHOLLS

Words on the Wind

The Tree and the Wind

'Where have you been?'
asked the tree of the wind;
'I've been to the North and the South, my friend;
I've been to the East and to the West,
to lands I like least
and some I like best.'

'What did you see?'
asked the tree of the wind;
'I saw many marvellous things, my friend;
I saw hungry people with empty hands
and others who died in foreign lands;
I saw the rich at table with sweet fruit to eat
and poor children with sores on their bleeding feet;
I saw forests of brown where nothing would grow
and farmers who had only dust to sow.'

'What did you hear?'
asked the tree of the wind;
'I heard both laughing and crying, my friend;
I head a dead sea crash on a black shore
and people's dry voices asking for more;
I heard the cry of the last bird on the wing
and the voice of a dumb child trying to sing;
I heard the sighing of water so still
and the sound of my own voice inside a hollow hill.'

'What did you feel?'
asked the tree of the wind;
'I felt great sorrow, deep sadness, my friend;
I felt my fingers freeze in the blue snow
and my arms burn in a red sun's glow;
I felt as though I was alone in the world
like someone who'd left a great story untold;
I felt that I had nowhere to turn,
nothing to do but depart and return.'

'And what did you do?'
asked the tree of the wind;
'What can any one of us do, my friend?
I just blew and I blew,
because that's what I do;
when it comes to the end
I am only the wind.'

ROBIN MELLOR

WORDS ON THE WIND

Old Man Ocean

Old Man Ocean, how do you pound
Smooth glass rough, rough stones round?
   Time and the tide and the wild waves rolling.
   Night and the wind and the long grey dawn.

Old Man Ocean, what do you tell,
What do you sing in the empty shell?
   Fog and the storm and the long bell tolling,
   Bones in the deep and the brave men gone.

RUSSELL HOBAN

Once the Wind

Once the wind
said to the sea
I am sad
        And the sea said
Why
        And the wind said
Because I
am not blue like the sky
or like you

        So the sea said what's
so sad about that
                  Lots
of things are blue
or red or other colours too
        but nothing
neither sea nor sky
can blow so strong
or sing so long as you

        And the sea looked sad
          So the wind said
Why

                              SHAKE KEANE

The West Wind

It's a warm wind, the west wind, full of birds' cries;
I never hear the west wind but tears are in my eyes.
For it comes from the west lands, the old brown hills,
And April's in the west wind, and daffodils.

It's a fine land, the west land, for hearts as tired as mine,
Apple orchards blossom there, and the air's like wine.
There is cool green grass there, where men may lie at rest,
And the thrushes are in song there, fluting from the nest.

'Will ye not come home, brother? ye have been long away,
It's April, and blossom time, and white is the may;
And bright is the sun, brother, and warm is the rain, –
Will ye not come home, brother, home to us again?

The young corn is green, brother, where the rabbits run,
It's blue sky, and white clouds, and warm rain and sun.
It's song to a man's soul, brother, fire to a man's brain,
To hear the wild bees and see the merry spring again.

Larks are singing in the west, brother, above the green wheat,
So will ye not come home, brother, and rest your tired feet?
I've a balm for bruised hearts, brother, sleep for aching eyes,'
Says the warm wind, the west wind, full of birds' cries.

WORDS ON THE WIND

It's the white road westwards is the road I must tread
To the green grass, the cool grass, and rest for heart and
    head
To the violets and the warm hearts and the thrushes' song,
In the fine land, the west land, the land where I belong.

JOHN MASEFIELD

Lady Moon

'I see the moon, and the moon sees me,
God bless the moon, and God bless me.'

Old Rhyme

Lady Moon, Lady Moon, where are you roving?
    Over the sea.
Lady Moon, Lady Moon, whom are you loving?
    All that love me.

Are you not tired with rolling, and never
    Resting to sleep?
Why look so pale and so sad, as forever
    Wishing to weep.

Ask me not this, little child, if you love me;
    You are too bold;
I must obey my dear Father above me,
    And do as I'm told.

Lady Moon, Lady Moon, where are you roving?
    Over the sea.
Lady Moon, Lady Moon, whom are you loving?
    All that love me.

LORD HOUGHTON

Day and Night

Said Day to Night,
'I bring God's light.
   What gift have you?'
   Night said, 'The dew.'

'I give bright hours,'
Quoth Day, 'and flowers.'
   Said Night, 'More blest,
   I bring sweet rest.'

LADY ANNE LINDSAY

A Conversation, from *Under Milk Wood*

      ROSIE PROBERT
What seas did you see,
Tom Cat, Tom Cat,
In your sailoring days
Long long ago?
What sea beasts were
In the wavery green
When you were my master?

      CAPTAIN CAT
I'll tell you the truth.
Seas barking like seals,
Blue seas and green,
Seas covered with eels
And mermen and whales.

      ROSIE
What seas did you sail
Old whaler when
On the blubbery waves
Between Frisco and Wales
You were my bosun?

      CAPTAIN CAT
As true as I'm here
You landlubber Rosie
You cosy love
My easy as easy
My true sweetheart,
Seas green as a bean
Seas gliding with swans
In the seal-barking moon.

DYLAN THOMAS

WORDS ON THE WIND

Song

'I like birds,' said the Dryad,
'and the murmuring of trees,
and stars seen through dark branches,
and mumbling, bumbling bees,
I like the forest and its smells and its shadows,
I like all of these.'

'I like fish,' said the Mermaid,
'and the sharp rustle of waves,
and the branching shapes of corals
that grow on seamen's graves,
I like the wetness and the depth and the silence,
I like green caves.'

ELIZABETH COATSWORTH

Christmas Scandal

'Christmas Tree,
   Green and white,
What do you say
   This festive night?'

'Nothing you'll like!
   What *can* I say?
The candles shine,
   The children play;

Nobody cares
   About my plight –
That any moment
   I'll catch alight!

Wax on my hair
   And round my throat,
Wax on my fine dark
   Winter coat;

Wax on my hips
   And tingling flanks,
Hot wax trickling
   Down my shanks . . . '

'Christmas Tree,
   Tall and spruce,
Keep your pecker up!'
   'What's the use?

Wax on my *toes* –
   But they're asleep,
Clamped in the flower-pot,
   Twisted deep!

A clumsy push,
   A flame, a scare
And they'll be dragging me
   By the hair!

They always forget,
   The stupid vandals!
That's why I say,
   "Blow the candles!"'

                              WILLIAM KEAN SEYMOUR

Snowman's Land

'Winds that blow, and the red sun low!
   Snowman, off to your bed – oh!
Where do you sleep when the shadows creep?'
   'High up here in the meadow.'

'Nuts to roast, with a bun to toast,
   And a supper of cake and spices;
But what's your fare in the field out there?'
   'Snow-water wine and ices.'

'A cage and bells, and a bird that tells
   Of tree-tops in the haven;
What bird is yours, from the misty moors?'
   'The black and brooding raven.'

'A dog to pat – and a tabby cat,
   With a miow-wow-a-wowling;
What's your pet, in the cold and wet?'
   'The prowling wolf-a-howling.'

'Who makes your bed by the embers red,
   With their soft little hush-a-bye-bye light?'
'The north wind blows me a sheet of snows,
   And hangs a star in the twilight.'

'A kiss for me – and it may be three,
   That never a mother misses;
Who kisses you in the icy dew?'
   'The silver moonbeam kisses.'

'And all the time, when the night bells chime,
   Do you dream – or dream you never?'
'I dream of the pole, where no bells toll,
   And a Snowman lives for ever.'

FLORENCE HARRISON

What Is Pink?

What is pink? a rose is pink
By the fountain's brink.
What is red? a poppy's red
In its barley bed.
What is blue? the sky is blue
Where the clouds float through.
What is white? a swan is white
Sailing in the light.
What is yellow? pears are yellow,
Rich and ripe and mellow.
What is green? the grass is green,
With small flowers between.
What is violet? clouds are violet
In the summer twilight.
What is orange? why, an orange,
Just an orange!

CHRISTINA ROSSETTI

The Clod and the Pebble

'Love seeketh not itself to please,
Nor for itself hath any care,
But for another gives its ease,
And builds a Heaven in Hell's despair.'

So sung a little Clod of Clay,
Trodden with the cattle's feet,
But a Pebble of the brook
Warbled out these metres meet:

'Love seeketh only Self to please,
To bind another to its delight,
Joys in another's loss of ease,
And builds a Hell in Heaven's despite.'

WILLIAM BLAKE

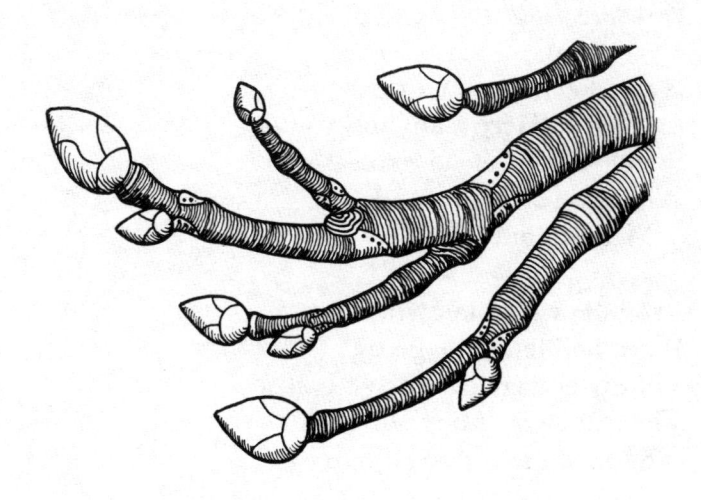

The Tree and the Pool

'I don't want my leaves to drop,' said the tree.
'I don't want to freeze,' said the pool.
'I don't want to smile,' said the sombre man.
'Or ever to cry,' said the Fool.

'I don't want to open,' said the bud.
'I don't want to end,' said the night.
'I don't want to rise,' said the neap-tide.
'Or ever to fall,' said the kite.

They wished and they murmured and whispered,
They said that to change was a crime.
Then a voice from nowhere answered,
'You must do what I say,' said Time.

BRIAN PATTEN

WORDS ON THE WIND

Waiting Both

A star looks down at me,
And says: 'Here I am and you
Stand each in our degree:
What do you mean to do, –
   Mean to do?'

I say: 'For all I know,
Wait, and let Time go by
Till my change comes.' – 'Just so',
The star says: 'So mean I: –
   So mean I.'

THOMAS HARDY

Heaven

O who will show me those delights on high?
   Echo.   I.
Thou Echo, thou art mortal, all men know.
   Echo.   No.
Wert thou not born among the trees and leaves?
   Echo.   Leaves.
And are there any leaves, that still abide?
   Echo.   Bide.
What leaves are they? impart the matter wholly.
   Echo.   Holy.
Are holy leaves the Echo then of bliss?
   Echo.   Yes.
Then tell me, what is that supreme delight?
   Echo.   Light.
Light to the mind: what shall the will enjoy?
   Echo.   Joy.
But are there cares and business with the pleasure?
   Echo.   Leisure.
Light, joy, and leisure; but shall they persevere?
   Echo.   Ever.

GEORGE HERBERT

What the Parents Said

Father and I in the Woods

'Son,'
My father used to say,
'Don't run.'

'Walk,'
My father used to say,
'Don't talk.'

'Words,'
My father used to say,
'Scare birds.'

So be:
It's sky and brook and bird
And tree.

DAVID MCCORD

A Lot to Ask

'Tell me, mother, how you bake this ham.'

    I put it in a slow heat,
    let the juices run,
    and in a little while it's done.

'How did you make my baby sleep?'

    I told her I was frightened of the dark,
    so she leaned across the rail,
    stroked and soothed me with a drowsy tale.

'Why, mother, are these sheets so soft?'

    I rest them on the breeze
    until they're warm against my skin
    – and then I fold them, bring them in.

'Your larder's empty, you've no coal.'

    I've potatoes in the attic,
    apples wrapped in straw,
    your father's thick socks from the war.

And harvest-time is coming.

JOHN LATHAM

WHAT THE PARENTS SAID

The Avaricious Boy

'Oh, see the sun above us shine.
I often wish it could be mine!'
Thus spoke the avaricious boy,
As though the sun were but a toy.
Explained his mother straightaway,
'The sun is not a thing of play,
And if this orb for which you yearn
Were given you, your hands would burn.
Far better we should wish for that
Which hurts us not – a ball to bat,
A kite to fly, a top to spin,
Or tiny soldiers made of tin.'
At this the avaricious boy
Commenced to clap and jump for joy,
And squealed, 'Mamma, the truth to tell,
I wish for all of those as well!'

COLIN WEST

A Conversation Overheard

No school today?

Oh yes school everyday
we play games and
sing and dance and
say ABC and add and
pray and fight and
paint and cry and laugh.

Do you like school?

No.

ANON

What Did You Learn in School Today

What did you learn in school today,
Dear little boy of mine?
What did you learn in school today,
Dear little boy of mine?
I learned that Washington never told a lie,
I learned that soldiers seldom die,
I learned that everybody's free,
That's what the teacher said to me,
And that's what I learned in school today,
That's what I learned in school.

What did you learn in school today,
Dear little boy of mine?
What did you learn in school today,
Dear little boy of mine?
I learned that policemen are my friends,
I learned that justice never ends,
I learned that murderers die for their crimes,
Even if we make a mistake sometimes,
And that's what I learned in school today,
That's what I learned in school.

What did you learn in school today,
Dear little boy of mine?
What did you learn in school today,
Dear little boy of mine?
I learned our government must be strong,
It's always right and never wrong,
Our leaders are the finest men,
And we elect them again and again,
And that's what I learned in school today,
That's what I learned in school.

What did you learn in school today,
Dear little boy of mine?
What did you learn in school today,
Dear little boy of mine?
I learned that war is not so bad,
I learned about the great ones we have had,
We fought in Germany and France,
And someday I might get my chance,
And that's what I learned in school today,
That's what I learned in school.

TOM PAXTON

Tell Me Why?

Daddy will you tell me why
There are no battleships in the sky?
   The reason is apparently
   They only battle on the sea

Then will you tell me if you please
Why grandfather clocks cannot sneeze?
   The reason is, or so I'm told
   They're too stupid and too old

Will you explain once and for all
Why little Jack Horner fell off the wall?
   It wasn't him it was little Bo Peep
   Now be a good boy and go to sleep

Daddy will you tell me when
Little boys grow into men?
   Some never do that's why they fight
   Now kiss me, let me hold you tight

For in the morning I must go
To join my regiment and so
   For Queen and country bravely die
   Son, oh son, please tell me why?

ROGER MCGOUGH

'Father, May I Go to War?'

'Father, may I go to war?'
'Yes, you may, my son,
But wear your woollen underwear,
And don't shoot off your gun.'

ANON

'Mother, May I Take a Swim?'

'Mother, may I take a swim?'
'Yes, my darling daughter,
But hang your clothes on a hickory limb,
And don't go near the water.'

ANON

Distracted the Mother Said to Her Boy

Distracted the mother said to her boy,
'Do you try to upset and perplex and annoy?
Now, give me four reasons – and don't play the fool –
Why you shouldn't get up and get ready for school.'

Her son replied slowly, 'Well, mother, you see,
I can't stand the teachers and they detest me;
And there isn't a boy or a girl in the place
That I like or, in turn, that delights in my face.'

'And I'll give you two reasons,' she said, 'why you ought
Get yourself off to school before you get caught;
Because, first, you are forty, and, next, you young fool,
It's your job to be there.
You're the head of the school.'

GREGORY HARRISON

Don't Go Through That Revolving Door

A: Don't go through that revolving door.
B: Why not?
A: My father's in it.
B: What's your father's name?
A: McGillacuddy.
B: Why, that's my name.
A: Father!
B: Son!

ANON

My Dad, Your Dad

My dad's fatter than your dad,
Yes, my dad's fatter than yours:
If he eats any more he won't fit in the house,
He'll have to live out of doors.

Yes, but my dad's balder than your dad,
My dad's balder, OK,
He's only got two hairs left on his head
And both are turning grey.

Ah, but my dad's thicker than your dad,
My dad's thicker, all right.
He has to look at his watch to see
If it's noon or the middle of the night.

Yes, but my dad's more boring than your dad.
If he ever starts counting sheep
When he can't get to sleep at night, he finds
It's the sheep that go to sleep.

But my dad doesn't mind your dad.
Mine quite likes yours too.
I suppose they don't always think much of US!
That's true, I suppose, that's true.

KIT WRIGHT

The Good Little Girl

It's funny how often they say to me, 'Jane?
   Have you been a *good* girl?'
   'Have you been a *good* girl?'
And when they have said it, they say it again,
   'Have you been a *good* girl?'
   'Have you been a *good* girl?'

I go to a party, I go out to tea,
I go to an aunt for a week at the sea,
I come back from school or from playing a game;
Wherever I come from, it's always the same:
   'Well?
Have you been a *good* girl, Jane?'

It's always the end of the loveliest day:
   'Have you been a *good* girl?'
   'Have you been a *good* girl?'
I went to the Zoo, and they waited to say:
   'Have you been a *good* girl?'
   'Have you been a *good* girl?'

Well, what did they think that I went there to do?
And why should I want to be bad at the Zoo?
And should I be likely to say if I had?
So that's why it's funny of Mummy and Dad,
This asking and asking, in case I was bad,
   'Well,
     Have you been a *good* girl, Jane?'

A. A. MILNE

The Spider

'Oh, look at that great ugly spider!' said Ann;
And screaming, she brushed it away with her fan;
''Tis a frightful black creature as ever can be,
I wish that it would not come crawling on me.'

'Indeed,' said her mother, 'I'll venture to say,
The poor thing will try to keep out of your way;
For after the fright, and the fall, and the pain,
It has much more occasion than you to complain.

But why should you dread the poor insect, my dear?
If it *hurt* you, there'd be some excuse for your fear;
But its little black legs, as it hurried away,
Did but tickle your arm as they went, I dare say.

For *them* to fear *us* we must grant to be just,
Who in less than a moment can tread them to dust;
But certainly *we* have no cause for alarm;
For, were they to try, they could do us no harm.

Now look! it has got to its home; do you see
What a delicate web it has spun in the tree?
Why here, my dear Ann, is a lesson for you:
Come learn from this spider what patience can do!

And when at your business you're tempted to play,
Recollect what you see in this insect to-day,
Or else, to your shame, it may seem to be true,
That a poor little spider is wiser than you.'

JANE TAYLOR

A Girl's Questions

   Mum,
where's my old doll,
the one that cried?
Where's my rocking horse,
and the garden slide?
   I don't know.

   Dad,
where's my jigsaw,
and my squeaky pram?
Where's old Panda
and my cuddly lamb?
   I don't know.

   Gran,
where's the dolls' house
Grandad built for me?
Where's the angel
from the Christmas tree?
   I don't know.

   Sad,
but I've outgrown them,
   I suppose.
I've put them aside
   like cast-off clothes.

   But
the saddest thing
   as older you grow
is to hear words like
   I don't know.

WES MAGEE

Slow Thaw

My daughter tells me of a dream she had.
'You were standing there.'
'What was I saying?'
'Nothing.'
'What was I doing?'
'Nothing.'
'Where was I?'
'I had a dream.'
She stands at the window looking out at the white garden
at the footprints that begin at the hedge
and go nowhere.
After a week of grey
the sky stretches blue to breaking point.
She's forgotten the dream.
She shows me a painting of someone in black.
'And who's this?' I ask, pointing to a blue lump,
several red lines in a corner.
'That's scribble,' she says,
'Just scribble',
Looking at me as if I should know.

IAN MCMILLAN

This Morning

The weathercock once again heading south
Catches the sun's eyes, and my daughter says
the blackbird has a crocus in its mouth.

'Spring's here,'
              I tell her.
                          'Here for always?'
'No, but for now.'
                  'Now is for always,
now is for always,'
                        she sings, as she takes
my hand and we take each other to school.

'I'll pick you some flowers and I'll make you cakes
and I'll swing in the sun all afternoon.'

WHAT THE PARENTS SAID

And I'll spend half the night with a worn pen
in that worn hand you're holding, one half-moon
eclipsed by a bruise, writing again
something I cannot say: that now is not
forever and to have is not to hold,
but they, you will learn, have nothing that
have nothing to lose. Your fingers unfold
their first delicate leaves. Among them, may
the bird in your hand set your veins singing
from moment to moment, always,
as mine do this morning.

JON STALLWORTHY

Little Abigail and the Beautiful Pony

There was a girl named Abigail
Who was taking a ride
Through the country
With her parents
When she spied a beautiful sad-eyed
Grey and white pony
And next to it was a sign
That said,
FOR SALE – CHEAP.
'Oh,' said Abigail,
'May I have that pony?
May I please?'
And her parents said,
'No you may not.'
And Abigail said,
'But I MUST have that pony.'
And her parents said,
'Well, you can't have that pony,
But you can have a nice butter pecan
Ice cream cone when we get home.'

And Abigail said,
'I don't want a butter pecan
Ice cream cone,
I WANT THAT PONY –
I MUST HAVE THAT PONY.'
And her parents said,
'Be quiet and stop nagging –
You're *not* getting that pony.'
And Abigail began to cry and said,
'If I don't get that pony I'll die.'

And her parents said, 'You won't die.
No child ever died yet from not getting a pony.'
And Abigail felt so bad
That when they got home she went to bed,
      And she couldn't eat,
      And she couldn't sleep,
      And her heart was broken,
      And she DID die –
      All because of a pony
      That her parents wouldn't buy.

      (This is a good story
      To read to your folks
      When they won't buy
      You something you want.)

SHEL SILVERSTEIN

Sailor

How long ago?

More than a hundred years.
He was your grandad's grandfather, you know.
His mother died when he was six years old.

And did he cry?

There would be tears.
So much remains untold.
Well-spoken, willing, trim,
at twelve he ran away,
shipped as a cabin boy, his letters say.

But why?

Oh, who can tell?
The sea encompassed him,
the brutish sea, its snarl his lullaby.
Sharp-slapping sail,
water and wind and sky
seasoned him well.
Teak hard and timber dry
he found odd harbourage between each gale,
for three decades scorched, froze
and then came home.

What did he bring?
A mermaid's comb?

Who knows?
A sea-salt thirst, tanned skin,
a knife scar down his side,
a coral spray, a ring –
but still within
his heart, so said his bride,
a gentleness. His mother's gift.
Who died.

MEG SEATON

Vision and Late Supper

Today my son asks me, 'What is a vision?'
I say, 'Blake saw God in a tree,
and his daddy beat him for telling lies.
That is a vision.'

I say, 'Your dad saw a ghost ship
passing his vessel
and dropping its cargo of peace.
That is a vision,

and different from having good vision.'
I say, 'Nero watched the slaughter
of Christians through a ruby
held close to his eye

not for good vision
but for good entertainment.'
I take off my glasses.
I say, 'Who taught you that word?'

And my son answers, 'I saw on TV
a boy like myself.
He held Superman in his hands
and Batman and Falcon and Angel,

and they obeyed him.
Today came a new man, very beautiful.
His name is Vision.
I am saving my money to buy

a Vision.' I say,
'If you can buy him
he's not a vision.
Not like your dad, who came to save me

from what some call solitude
and some call grief.
Not like you, thief of our faces
yet wholly your own,

two stars to wish on,
that rise from this table like morning.'

NANCY WILLARD

From a Very Little Sphinx

I

Come along in then, little girl!
Or else stay out!
But in the open door she stands,
And bites her lip and twists her hands,
And stares upon me, trouble-eyed:
'Mother,' she says, 'I can't decide!
I can't decide!'

EDNA ST VINCENT MILLAY

WHAT THE PARENTS SAID

The Room

'Child! Child! Come along in!
Old Sun's at downfall,
time you were in bed,
or you'll miss the light on the wall
that you so love.'

'I came in long ago,
I never miss the light on the wall
that I so love.
I never shall.'

FRANCES BELLERBY

The Sick Child

'O mother, lay your hand on my brow!
O mother, mother, where am I now?
Why is the room so gaunt and great?
Why am I lying awake so late?'

'Fear not at all: the night is still.
Nothing is here that means you ill –
Nothing but lamps the whole town through,
And never a child awake but you.'

'Mother, mother, speak low in my ear,
Some of the things are so great and near,
Some are so small and far away,
I have a fear that I cannot say.
What have I done, and what do I fear,
And why are you crying, mother dear?'

'Out in the city, sounds begin.
Thank the kind God, the carts come in!
An hour or two more, and God is so kind,
The day shall be blue in the window-blind,
Then shall my child go sweetly asleep,
To dream of the birds and the hills of sheep.'

ROBERT LOUIS STEVENSON

Uphill

Does the road wind uphill all the way?
    Yes, to the very end.
Will the day's journey take the whole long day?
    From morn to night, my friend.

But is there for the night a resting-place?
    A roof for when the slow, dark hours begin.
May not the darkness hide it from my face?
    You cannot miss that inn.

Shall I meet other wayfarers at night?
    Those who have gone before.
Then must I knock, or call when just in sight?
    They will not keep you waiting at that door.

Shall I find comfort, travel-sore and weak?
    Of labour you shall find the sum.
Will there be beds for me and all who seek?
    Yea, beds for all who come.

CHRISTINA ROSSETTI

*This book is dedicated
with love
to the unforgettable*

WEDNESDAY GROUP
Jo
Paul
Kate
Zoë
Julian
Lindsey
Nick
Matthew
and
Charlotte

You would have spoken and acted these poems with the expression and enthusiasm you gave to 'The Giggle', 'The Itch', 'St George and the Dragon' and so much else . . . and now perhaps your children will.

Acknowledgements

The author and the publisher would like to thank the following for their kind permission to reprint copyright material in this book:

The Estate of Reginald Arkell for 'The Lady of Shalots' by Reginald Arkell, from *Greenfingers* (Hutchinson); Faber and Faber Ltd for 'O What Is That Sound' by W.H. Auden from *Collected Poems* (Faber and Faber Ltd); David Higham Associates for 'The Room' by Frances Bellerby from *Selected Poems* (Enitharmon Press, 1986); Catherine Benson for 'David and Goliath' by Catherine Benson, copyright © 1993 Catherine Benson; Gerard Benson for 'Overheard in a Doctor's Waiting-room' by Gerard Benson, copyright © 1988 Gerard Benson, first published 1988 in *New Statesman and Society*; 'How to Treat Elves' by Morris Bishop reprinted by permission of the Putnam Publishing Group from *Spilt Milk* by Morris Bishop. Copyright © 1942 by Morris Bishop. Renewed © 1969 by Morris Bishop; Faber and Faber Ltd for 'Ruth Luce and Bruce Booth' by N.M. Bodecker from *Snowman Sniffles* (Faber and Faber Ltd, 1983); David Higham Associates for 'Mary, Mary Magdalene' by Charles Causley from *Figgie Hobbin*; Blackwell Publishers for 'Noah and the Rabbit' by Hugh Chesterman, copyright © 1974 Hugh Chesterman; Christopher Cornford as Literary Executor for Frances Cornford for 'The Night Express' by Frances Cornford, from *Collected Poems* (Cressett Press, 1954); 'Some Curious Habits of Jonathan Bing' by Beatrice Curtis Brown from *Jonathan Bing*, copyright © 1936, © 1968 by Beatrice Curtis Brown, reproduced by permission of Curtis Brown, London; Coward-McCann, Inc. for 'The Barn' by Elizabeth Coatsworth, reprinted by permission of Coward-McCann, Inc. from *Compass Rose* By Elizabeth Coatsworth, copyright © 1929 by Coward-McCann, Inc. Copyright renewed © 1957 by Elizabeth Coatsworth. The Estate of Elizabeth Coatsworth for 'On a Night of Snow' from *Night and the Cat of Snow* by Elizabeth Coatsworth. 'Song' by Elizabeth Coatsworth reprinted with permission of Macmillan Publishing Company from *Summer Green* by Elizabeth Coatsworth. Copyright © 1948 by Macmillan Publishing Company, renewed 1976 by Elizabeth Coatsworth Beston; The Reverend Hopkinson for the extract '*from* Little Mary Crosbie' by Margaret Cropper, from *Poems by Margaret Cropper* (1983); The Literary Trustees of Walter de la Mare and The Society of Authors as their representative for 'Bones' and 'Bunches of Grapes' from *Songs of Childhood* by Walter de la Mare; Jan Dean for 'Catching a Carp' by Jan Dean, copyright © 1993 Jan Dean; B.D. Bartlett for 'Conversation' by Olive Dove from *Drumming in the Sky* (BBC Books, 1981) and 'Let Us In' by Olive Dove from *Witch Words* (Faber and Faber Ltd, 1987), both copyright B.D. Bartlett; David Durham for 'Daydreamer' by David Durham, copyright © David Durham; The Lutterworth Press, Cambridge for 'Café Conversation' by Richard Edwards,

ACKNOWLEDGEMENTS

copyright © 1987 Richard Edwards; The Watts Publishing Group for 'Lost and Found' by Richard Edwards from *A Mouse in My Roof* (Orchard Books, 1988); David Higham Associates for 'Meeting Mary' by Eleanor Farjeon from *Silver Sand and Snow* (Michael Joseph); The Estate of Robert Frost for 'The Telephone' by Robert Frost from *The Poetry of Robert Frost*, edited by Edward Connery Lathem (Jonathan Cape); The Society of Authors as the literary representative of the Estate of Rose Fyleman for 'Witch, Witch' by Rose Fyleman; A.P. Watt Ltd on behalf of The Trustees of the Robert Graves Copyright Trust for 'A Frosty Night' taken from *Collected Poems* (1975) by Robert Graves; Gregory Harrison for 'Distracted the Mother Said to Her Boy' by Gregory Harrison, copyright © Gregory Harrison, from *A Fourth Poetry Book* (Oxford University Press); David Higham Associates for 'Old Man Ocean' by Russell Hoban from *The Pedalling Man* (Heineman); 'Interview With a Poet' by Miroslav Holub from *Notes of a Clay Pigeon*, copyright © 1977 Miroslav Holub, translation copyright © 1977 Ian Jarmila Milner, reprinted by permission of Martin Secker and Warburg Limited; 'Vermont Conversation' reprinted with permission of Atheneum Publishers, an imprint of Macmillan Publishing Company, from *The Apple Vendor's Fair* by Patricia Hubbell. Copyright © 1963, renewed 1991, by Patricia Hubbell; Serpent's Tail, 4 Blackstock Mews, London N4 2BT for 'Early Evening Quarrel' and 'Madam and the Rent Man' by Langston Hughes from *Selected Poems*, copyright © 1959 Langston Hughes (Pluto Press, 1986); Shake Keane for 'Once the Wind', copyright © 1988 Shake Keane, from *Black Poetry* (Blackie Children's Books); David King for 'To My Dog Brock' by David King, copyright © 1993 David King; John Latham for 'A Lot to Ask' by John Latham, copyright © 1985 John Latham, from *The Other Side of the Street* (Peterloo Poets, 1985); McLelland and Stewart Ltd for 'The Well-wrought Urn' by Irving Layton from *The Darkening Fire* (Poems 1945–1968); Rand McNally and Company for 'Hallowe'en' by Marie A. Lawson from *Child Life* magazine, copyright © 1936, 1964 by Rand McNally and Company; Naomi Lewis for 'A Footprint on the Air' by Naomi Lewis, copyright © Naomi Lewis; Maurice Lindsay for '999', copyright © Maurice Lindsay, from *Collected Poems (1940–1990)*; Houghton Mifflin Company for 'In the East' from *Seeing, Collected Poems 1917–1982* by Archibald MacLeish. Copyright © 1985 by The Estate of Archibald MacLeish. Reprinted by permission of Houghton Mifflin Company. All rights reserved; Wes Magee for 'A Girl's Questions' by Wes Magee, copyright © 1989 Wes Magee, from *Morning Break and Other Poems* by Wes Magee (Cambridge University Press, 1989); The Society of Authors as the literary representative of the Estate of John Masefield for 'The West Wind' by John Masefield; Hannah McBain for 'My Very Peculiar Pet' by Hannah McBain; Chambers Publishers for 'Jam' and 'Father and I in the Woods' by David McCord from *Mr Bidery's Spidery Garden*; 'Tell Me Why?' by Roger McGough from *Pie in the Sky* (Kestrel Books), reprinted by permission of the Peters, Fraser & Dunlop Group Ltd; Ian McMillan for 'Slow Thaw' by Ian McMillan, copyright © 1988 Ian McMillan, first published 1988 by

ACKNOWLEDGEMENTS

Wine Skin Press; Robin Mellor for 'The Tree and the Wind' by Robin Mellor, copyright © 1993 Robin Mellor, reprinted by permission of the author, first appeared February 1993 in *Welsh Rhubarb* by Robin Mellor (Victoria Press); Marian Reiner for 'Teevee' from *Jamboree Rhymes for All Times* by Eve Merriam, copyright © 1962, 1964, 1966, 1973, 1984 by Eve Merriam. Reprinted by permission of Marian Reiner; Methuen Children's Books for 'The Good Little Girl' by A.A. Milne from *Now We are Six*, copyright © 1989 by Methuen Children's Books; Carcanet Press for 'The First Men on Mercury' by Edwin Morgan from *Glasgow to Saturn* (Carcanet Press); Faber and Faber Ltd for 'Storytime' by Judith Nicholls from *Midnight Forest* (Faber and Faber Ltd, 1987); Rogers, Coleridge and White for 'This and That', copyright © 1988 by Gareth Owen from *Salford Road and Other Poems* (Young Lions, 1988); Viking Children's Books for 'You Can't Be That' from *Thawing Frozen Frogs* by Brian Patten and 'The Tree and the Pool' by Brian Patten from *Gargling With Jelly* © Brian Patten, 1985; Margaret Porter for 'Are You Receiving Me?', copyright © 1993 by Margaret Porter; The Laura Cecil Literary Agency for 'Cows' by James Reeves, copyright © James Reeves from *The Wandering Moon and Other Poems* (Puffin Books) by James Reeves, reprinted by permission of the James Reeves Estate; Richard Rieu for the Estate of the late E.V. Rieu for 'The Flattered Flying-Fish' from *The Flattered Flying-Fish and Other Poems* by E.V. Rieu (Methuen, 1962); David Higham Associates for 'Gargoyles' from *The Cathedral* and 'Unwelcome Guest' from *The Golden Unicorn* by Clive Sansom and published by Methuen; Vernon Scannell for 'Youth, Age and Poetry: A Dialogue' by Vernon Scannell from *Winterlude* (Robson Books, 1982), copyright © 1982 Vernon Scannell; Peterloo Poets for 'Sailor' by Meg Seaton from *Party People* (Peterloo Poets, 1984); Ian Serraillier for 'What's the Problem?', copyright © 1993 Ian Serraillier, and 'The Tickle Rhyme', copyright © 1950 Ian Serraillier; Edite Kroll Literary Agency for 'Little Abigail and the Beautiful Pony' from *A Light in the Attic* by Shel Silverstein. Copyright © 1981 by Evil Eye Music, Inc.; 'Her-zie' by Stevie Smith reprinted by permission of James MacGibbon from *The Collected Poems of Stevie Smith* (Penguin 20th Century Classics), copyright © 1975 James MacGibbon; Harriet Wasserman Literary Agency for 'Raccoon' by William Jay Smith from *Boy Blue's Book of Beasts*; Elizabeth Barnett for 'From a Very Little Sphinx' by Edna St Vincent Millay. From *Collected Poems* HarperCollins. Copyright © 1929, 1956 by Edna St Vincent Millay and Norma Millay Ellis. Reprinted by permission of Elizabeth Barnett, literary executor; Jonathan Cape for 'This Morning' by Jon Stallworthy from *Hand in Hand* (Jonathan Cape); David Higham Associates for 'A Conversation' by Dylan Thomas from *Under Milk Wood* (J.M. Dent); Barrie Wade for 'Studup', copyright © 1991 by Barrie Wade, from *Barley, Barley* (Oxford University Press, 1991); Colin West for 'Lanky Lee and Lindy Lou' and 'The Avaricious Boy', copyright © 1992 Colin West; Harcourt Brace Jovanovich for 'Vision and Late Supper' by Nancy Willard from *Household Tales of Moon and Water* (Harcourt Brace Jovanovich, 1975); 'The Traveller'

ACKNOWLEDGEMENTS

by Raymond Wilson from *Time's Delights* (Paul Hamlyn, 1977), copyright © Raymond Wilson, and 'Grave Talk' by Raymond Wilson from *To Be a Ghost* (Viking, 1991), copyright © Raymond Wilson; Lions, an imprint of HarperCollins Publishers Limited for 'My Dad, Your Dad', and 'Ghosts' copyright © 1978 Kit Wright from *Rabbiting On*.

Every effort has been made to trace the copyright holders, but the author and publisher apologize if any inadvertent omission has been made.

Fairfield P.N.E.U. School
(Backwell) Ltd.,
Farleigh Road,
Backwell, Bristol.